OXFORD MEDICAL PUBLICATIONS

Obsessive–Compulsive Disorder

THE FACTS

Donated by
Cumberland County Mental Health
Department

Obsessive–Compulsive Disorder

THE FACTS

PADMAL DE SILVA

Institute of Psychiatry, University of London
Bethlem Royal and Maudsley Hospitals, London

and

STANLEY RACHMAN

Psychology Department, University of
British Columbia, Vancouver

OXFORD NEW YORK TOKYO
OXFORD UNIVERSITY PRESS

Oxford University Press, Walton Street, Oxford OX2 6DP

Oxford New York
Athens Auckland Bangkok Bombay
Calcutta Cape Town Dar es Salaam Delhi
Florence Hong Kong Istanbul Karachi
Kuala Lumpur Madras Madrid Melbourne
Mexico City Nairobi Paris Singapore
Taipei Tokyo Toronto
and associated companies in
Berlin Ibadan

Oxford is a trade mark of Oxford University Press

Published in the United States by
Oxford University Press Inc., New York

© Padmal de Silva and Stanley Rachman, 1992

First published 1992
Reprinted 1992, 1993, 1995

A catalogue record for this book is available from the British Library

Library of Congress Cataloging in Publication Data
De Silva, Padmal.
Obsessive compulsive disorder : the facts / Padmal de Silva and
Stanley Rachman.
p. cm.—(Oxford medical publications)
Includes index.
1. Obsessive-compulsive disorder—Popular works. ·I. Rachman,
Stanley. II. Title. III. Series.
[DNLM: 1. Obsessive-Compulsive Disorder. WM 176 D611o]
RC533.D4 1992 616.85'227—dc20 88-636438
ISBN 0-19-262153-X
ISBN 0-19-262188-2 (pbk.)

Printed and bound in Great Britain by
Biddles Ltd, Guildford and King's Lynn

Preface

This book is intended to provide the reader with basic information about obsessive–compulsive disorder. This is a relatively common neurotic disorder seen in clinics and hospitals, and is more widespread than had been traditionally assumed. Some recent surveys have shown a lifetime prevalence rate of up to three per cent in the general population. It is only the more severely afflicted, however, who come for help.

We have been involved in the study and treatment of obsessive–compulsive patients for many years. In our clinical practice, we have found the lack of a basic book to be recommended to sufferers and their families to be a major handicap. We hope that sufferers of the disorder, and their families and friends, will find these pages of some use. We also hope that the general reader interested in finding out about this fascinating disorder will find this book useful.

Research in the last twenty-five years has thrown much light on this condition, and we have attempted to give a summary of some of these findings. A great deal more is known about this disorder than was understood in the 1950s or the 1960s, but there remain many unanswered questions. We have deliberately refrained from attempting to provide simple answers to these questions; to have done so would have been misleading.

Much of what is said about the treatment of obsessive–compulsive disorder in this book reflects a psychological orientation. This is partly because of our own professional training but, more importantly, because the psychological approach has provided the most effective therapeutic strategies to help those who have these problems. Current and future research will no doubt lead to the refinement of the existing treatment strategies and the development of new ones. It will also throw more light on aetiology and other questions. Like everyone else interested in this area, we eagerly await these developments.

NOTE

Because of the problem of gender in the English language, we have had to decide whether to use 'he', 'she', or 'person' when referring to people. Different authors have different practices, and we are aware that some people have strong views on this issue. For ease of reading, we have retained the more conventional, male form.

London and   P. de S.
Vancouver   S.R.
August 1991

Acknowledgements

There are several people to whom we wish to express our gratitude. Tania Deans, Jean Morgan, and Moira Hall gave excellent secretarial help. Valuable editorial advice was given, at various stages, by the staff of Oxford University Press. A number of our colleagues, over the years, have contributed much to our work and thinking on the subject covered in this book. We should particularly like to mention Ray Hodgson, Lesley Parkinson, Helen Likierman, Gisela Roper, Gudrun Sartory, Ian Jakes, and Melanie Marks.

Contents

1. An introduction to obsessive–compulsive disorder

Obsessive–compulsive disorder is traditionally regarded as a neurotic disorder, like phobias and anxiety states. Other terms used for this disorder include 'obsessive (or obsessional)–compulsive neurosis' and 'obsessive (or obsessional)–compulsive illness'—or simply 'obsessive (or obsessional) disorder' or 'compulsive disorder'. People with this problem can suffer considerable distress, and often feel that they are helpless victims. Although neurotic disorders are generally considered to be less handicapping and disabling than psychotic illnesses—such as schizophrenia—severe obsessive–compulsive disorder sometimes causes major incapacitation and drastically affects people's lives.

Perhaps a brief note is necessary about the terms 'neurotic disorder' and 'psychotic disorder'. Broadly speaking, neurotic disorders, or neuroses, are relatively minor psychiatric illnesses. The neurotic patient is aware that he has a problem—that is, he has insight. His contact with the outside world is relatively intact. In contrast, psychotic disorders, or psychoses, are more serious mental illnesses. The psychotic patient may have no insight that something is wrong with him, and his contact with the outside world may be severely impaired.

In current psychiatric thinking, obsessive–compulsive disorder is classified as an anxiety disorder. Other anxiety disorders include phobias, panic disorder, and generalized anxiety; they all share anxiety as a basic feature, and there is overlap of symptoms among them.

What is meant when someone is described as having an obsessive–compulsive disorder? The person displays and/or complains of either obsessions or compulsions or both, to a degree that affects his everyday functioning or causes him distress. Psychiatric diagnosis of the condition is usually made on this basis. This is reflected in the generally agreed diagnostic criteria (Table 1).

Table 1. Summary of criteria widely used for the diagnosis of obsessive–compulsive disorder

---

1. The person must have either obsessions or compulsions or both.
    (a) *Obsessions* are recurrent, persistent ideas, thoughts, images, or impulses that intrude into consciousness and are experienced as senseless or repugnant. They form against one's will, and the person attempts to resist them, or get rid of them. The person recognizes that they are his own thoughts, and so on.
    (b) *Compulsions* are repetitive, purposeful forms of behaviour that are carried out because of a strong feeling of compulsion to do so, and are usually performed according to certain rules or in a stereotyped fashion. The behaviour is not an end in itself, but is aimed at producing or preventing some event or situation. However, the activity is not connected in a realistic way with what it is aimed to produce or prevent, or it is clearly excessive. The person generally recognizes the senselessness of the behaviour and does not get any pleasure from carrying out the activity, although it provides a relief from tension.

2. They are not due to another disorder, such as schizophrenia, depression, or organic mental disorder.

3. The obsessions and/or compulsions cause distress to the person and/or interfere with his life and activities.

WHAT ARE OBSESSIONS?

An obsession is an unwanted, intrusive, recurrent, and persistent thought, image, or impulse. Obsessions are not voluntarily produced, but are experienced as events that invade a person's consciousness. They can be worrying, repugnant, blasphemous, obscene, nonsensical, or all of these. The person neither wants nor welcomes them; instead, he usually resists them and tries to get rid of them. An obsession is a passive experience: it happens to the person. He may be engaged in some activity, like reading a book or driving a car, when the obsession intrudes into his consciousness. It disrupts his normal thinking and behaviour.

Some examples of obsessions are as follows:

1. A young woman had the recurrent intrusive thought that her husband would die in a car crash. She also had vivid visual imagery

accompanying this thought: she would 'see' the scene of the accident, the two cars, the broken glass, the blood, and the injured.

2. A young woman had the recurrent intrusive thought that she was contaminated by dirt and germs from strangers.

3. A man had the recurrent intrusive doubt that he may have knocked down someone crossing the road.

4. A young married woman had the recurrent intrusive impulse to strangle children and domestic animals. This would be followed by the thought or doubt that she might actually have done this.

5. A young man had the recurrent intrusive thought 'Christ was a bastard'. He also felt an impulse to shout this out during prayer or a church service.

6. A young woman had the recurrent intrusive thought 'Am I a lesbian?'.

7. A young man had recurrent intrusive images of himself violently attacking, with an axe, his elderly parents. He also had the thought that he might actually commit this act. This experience included images of the victims, of blood flowing, and of injuries caused.

8. A young woman had the recurrent, intrusive impulse to harm herself by burning her eyes with a lighted cigarette. This was accompanied by visual images of the act.

9. A middle-aged man had the recurrent thought that he had cancer, or would develop cancer.

10. A fourteen-year-old girl had the recurrent impulse to blurt out obscenities in public. She also had the thought that she might actually do, or have done, this.

These examples show the main features of an obsession. It intrudes into consciousness, as an unwelcome outsider. It may take the form of a thought, an image, an impulse, or a combination of these. Obsessions in the form of thoughts are much more common than those in the form of impulses or images. When the obsession occurs, the person usually resists it, and tries to dismiss it. If he succeeds in dismissing it, it may well come back within a short period of time. Some patients report that their obsessions are with them most of their waking hours, despite desperate struggles to get rid of them. The effort involved in attempting to subdue obsessions can be exhausting, even though the struggle is not evident to friends or relatives.

The patient does not regard the obsessional thought, image, or impulse as something originating from outside: he recognizes and acknowledges that it is his own thought. This is an important feature as, in certain mental illnesses, patients may have the experience of thoughts having been put into their heads by outside agents. Obsessions are not experienced in this way.

Different uses of the word 'obsession'

It should be noted that the meaning of the term 'obsession' in the context of obsessive–compulsive disorder is different from how the word is used in day-to-day language. We often hear someone being described as 'obsessed with his job', and expressions such as 'He is obsessed with her', 'Football is an obsession for him', and so on. What is meant in such instances is that the person in question has an unusually great interest in something or someone, so that everything else pales into insignificance. But such an attachment, interest, or preoccupation is not seen by him as unwanted or unacceptable, and there is no resistance or any attempt to dismiss it. Nor is it something that keeps intruding episodically into the person's mind. This is very different from the way the term 'obsession' is used in reference to obsessive–compulsive disorder. Both senses are related to the meaning of the Latin verb *obsidere* ('to besiege') from which the word 'obsession' is derived.

What are obsessions about?

What are the contents of obsessions? There are some very common themes. Contamination and dirt; disease and illness; death, violence, and aggression; harm and danger; and moral and religious topics feature prominently among them. There are also sex-related obsessions and, less commonly, entirely senseless or trivial ones. An example of one of the latter came from a man who complained of the recurrent, intrusive thought: 'These boys when they were young'. A woman had intrusive visual images of asymmetrical objects and patterns she had seen, which would repeatedly come to her. In some cases, the obsession consists of a doubting thought, which can apply to most things that the person does. For example, a young woman complained that, whenever she performed any action, she would immediately be assailed by the thought 'Did I do it right?' or 'Have I done the right thing?'.

WHAT ARE COMPULSIONS?

A compulsion is a repetitive and seemingly purposeful behaviour that is performed according to certain rules or in a stereotyped fashion. It may be wholly unacceptable or, more often, partly acceptable. The behaviour is not an end in itself, but is usually intended to produce, or to prevent, some event or situation. However, the activity is not connected in a logical or realistic way with what it is intended to achieve (for example touching a relative's photograph a certain number of times, in order to ensure that no harm comes to the relative), or it may be clearly excessive (such as washing hands for half-an-hour at a time to get rid of germs). There are also instances where the person engages in the compulsive act simply to ward off great anxiety, or even panic. The act is preceded or accompanied by a sense of subjective compulsion—that is, the person feels a strong urge to engage in the behaviour. Usually, there is a desire to resist. The person recognizes the senselessness or irrationality of the behaviour, and does not derive any pleasure from carrying it out, although it provides a release of tension or a feeling of relief in the short term.

Some examples of compulsions are as follows:

1. A young woman repeatedly and extensively washed her hands to get rid of contamination by germs. The washing was done in an elaborate ritual, six times without soap and six times with soap, on each occasion.
2. A young man checked door handles, gas taps, and electric switches every time he went past them.
3. A 15-year-old girl cleaned and washed the area around her bed, including the wall, every night before going to bed, in order to rid it of germs and dirt.
4. A man opened letters he had written and sealed, to make sure that he had written the correct things. Thus he would rip open the envelope, reread the letter, and put it into a new one, several times before posting it.
5. A woman in her forties complained that every time she entered a room, she had to touch the four corners of it, starting from the left.
6. A young man had the compulsion to touch with the left hand anything he had touched with the right hand, and vice versa.

7. A young man had the compulsion to empty his bladder before each meal. Even if he had urinated a short while before, he would go and empty his bladder prior to sitting down to the meal. He felt that otherwise he would not be able to enjoy his meal.

8. A young man had the compulsion to look back over his shoulder at any building that he was leaving. He would first look back over his left shoulder, then over his right, and then again over the left.

9. A young woman had the compulsion to wipe, with a wet cloth, all tables and worktops several times each time that she was to use them. She did this to get rid of what she called 'invisible food particles'.

10. A 35-year-old married woman had the compulsion to wash and disinfect herself and her clothes, out of fear of contracting cancer. She spent many hours each day doing this.

The key feature of all these examples is that the person feels a strong urge—a compulsive urge—to engage in a particular behaviour, which he carries out despite resistance and despite recognizing that it is irrational or at least excessive.

Covert compulsions

All the examples cited above are of overt compulsive behaviour—that is, behaviour involving bodily actions; but some compulsions are covert, or mental. Unfortunately, many writers on obsessive–compulsive disorder, and many doctors, psychologists, and psychiatrists, tend to assume that compulsions are necessarily overt behaviour. They consider obsessions to be mental events, and compulsions to be overt, motor, events. This division is incorrect. It is certainly true that obsessions are mental events, but not all compulsions are motor behaviour. Many patients have covert, or mental, compulsions which have all the main features of overt compulsions.

Here are some examples:

1. A man had the compulsion to say silently a certain string of words, whenever he heard or read of any disaster or accident.

2. A middle-aged woman, who was distressed by the intensive repetitive appearance in her consciousness of obscene words, carried out a compulsive ritual each time this happened. This consisted of changing these words into similar acceptable ones—for example, 'well' for 'hell'—and saying them silently four times.

3. A middle-aged man had the compulsion to visualize everything that was said in conversation to him, and what he was going to say in reply. He would not reply until he had obtained these visual images.

4. A woman, who was tormented by intrusive repetitions of bloody images of her relations and friends, felt compelled to re-form those images, with the people concerned in good health.

5. A young woman became very worried if she set her eyes on black objects, especially before going to sleep. When this happened, she had the obsessional thought that it would cause her to go blind, or lead to some other disaster. So, every time she experienced this, she felt compelled to visualize an object of a different colour, especially white, as a way of preventing these ill effects.

These examples should make it clear that compulsions are not exclusively motor behaviour, but can be mental acts as well. Covert compulsions are also referred to as 'cognitive rituals' or 'cognitive compulsions'.

The active nature of compulsions

A feature of compulsions that needs to be stressed here is that a compulsion is actively brought about by the patient: he is not happy about doing it, but it is essentially his voluntary action, performed as a result of his compulsive urge, and not an automatic behaviour. Thus, it is different from tics and muscle spasms that are found in some people, especially children, which are essentially involuntary motor responses. These are not actively produced by the patient, making them different from compulsions.

Resistance

Obsessions and compulsions are generally resisted. At one time, it was considered by many experts that resistance was an essential feature of obsessive–compulsive disorder. However, we now know that this is not the case. Although in the vast majority of cases the person does resist the obsession or the compulsive urge, there are many exceptions, particularly with regard to compulsions. It appears that in the early stages of the disorder a patient resists his compulsive urges strenuously, but after repeated failures over a period time, he may begin to show much less resistance. Patients with chronic obsessive–compulsive problems may experience little or no resistance to the obsessions or the urges.

Different uses of the word 'compulsion'

As with the term 'obsession', our use of the term 'compulsion' here is different from and more specific than the way it is used in everyday language. We often hear people talking about 'compulsive lying', 'compulsive eating', 'compulsive gambling', and so on. These types of behaviour are different from the kinds of compulsions that we are concerned with here. As noted above, compulsions are acts which are the result of an urge that the person usually tries to resist, and which are carried out reluctantly. They are seen as essentially irrational or senseless, and give no pleasure or satisfaction. Forms of behaviour such as compulsive gambling do not show these features—although they are problems in their own right, they are not part of obsessive–compulsive disorder.

Sometimes the term 'compulsive' is used for behaviour such as recurrent nail-biting, thumb-sucking, and hair-pulling. These are habits, and the person usually engages in them, at least part of the time, without being aware of them. They lack the characteristic features of the compulsion in obsessive–compulsive disorder, such as purposefulness and meaningfulness. True compulsions are carried out in order to accomplish some aim; behaviour such as nail-biting, hair-pulling, and so on is not. Nor do they provoke a feeling of resistance. These kinds of behaviour are best seen as habits rather than true compulsions, as their similarity to the latter is superficial.

THE DIAGNOSIS OF OBSESSIVE–COMPULSIVE DISORDER

We noted, in an earlier section, that someone may be considered to have an obsessive–compulsive disorder if he experiences or displays obsessions or compulsions, or both (see pp. 1–2). However, we added an important qualification: it is not the presence of obsessions and/or compulsions as such that matters, but the degree to which they cause distress and/or interfere with the person's life. This is an additional requirement in the diagnostic criteria cited in Table 1 (see p. 2). In the following paragraphs, we shall try to make clear why this qualification is necessary.

Obsessions and compulsions in the general population

It is important to realize that obsessions and compulsions are not uncommon in the general population—there are many people who never go to a clinic or hospital seeking help, but who have obsessions and/or compulsions.

Normal obsessions

Several research studies carried out in different centres have shown that many people randomly selected from the general population, in fact about four-fifths of them, have obsessions. These are no different in either form or content from the obsessions of patients who seek help. The differences are quantitative: the non-patients tend to have them less frequently, their distress as a result of them is less severe, and so on. In a study that was carried out in London some years ago, we asked a random sample of people to report their obsessions, if they had any. Here are some of the obsessions they described.

- thought of accident occurring to a loved one;
- thought of harm befalling her children, especially accidents;
- thought that the chances of an air crash involving herself would be minimized if one of her relatives had such an accident;
- thought that she might commit suicide;
- thought of 'unnatural' sexual acts;
- impulse to jump off the platform in front of approaching train;
- impulse to violently attack and kill a dog;
- impulse to do something (for example, shout, or throw things) to disrupt peace at a gathering;
- thought that she and her husband and the baby she was due to have would be greatly harmed because of exposure to asbestos.

As can be seen, they are similar to the obsessions commonly reported by obsessive–compulsive patients.

Normal compulsions

Similarly, a large proportion of normal people have compulsions. Various forms of checking behaviour are quite commonplace. Consider, for example, a man who goes round the house checking to make sure that all gas taps are closed, before leaving home; or a housewife who goes back once or twice to the kitchen she has just left in order to check that the oven is switched off. No-one would seriously consider them to have an obsessive–compulsive disorder requiring help. Many people have minor compulsive rituals, such as always putting on the left shoe first, or arranging the desk in a certain way. Studies have shown that such compulsions are not uncommon in the general population.

An excellent account of a compulsion in a normal person is provided in Boswell's biography of Samuel Johnson, the great eighteenth century man of letters. Boswell commented on various 'singularities' or 'particularities' of Johnson.

He had another particularity, of which none of his friends ever ventured to ask an explanation. It appeared to be some superstitious habit, which he had contracted early, and from which he had never called upon his reason to disentangle him. This was his anxious care to go out or in at a door or passage by a certain number of steps from a certain point, or at least so as that either his right or his left foot (I am not certain which) should constantly make the first actual movement when he came close to the door or passage. Thus I conjecture: for I have upon innumerable occasions, observed him suddenly stop, and then seem to count his steps with a deep earnestness; and when he had neglected or gone wrong in this sort of magical movement, I have seen him go back again, put himself in a proper position to begin the ceremony, and, having gone through it, break from his abstraction, walk briskly on, and join his companion.

Superstitions

There are similarities between superstitious ideas and some obsessions, and between superstitious acts and compulsive behaviour. Superstitions and certain obsessions are similar in that the person recognizes the irrationality of the idea or its associated activity, but prefers to err on the side of caution or safety. Like compulsions, many superstitious acts are carried out in order to prevent a misfortune from happening. However, there are also many superstitious acts that are carried out in order to enhance the probability of good fortune; this is never the case with compulsive behaviour. Further, obsessions can be distinguished from most superstitions in that the content of the obsession is often unacceptable or repugnant, leads to resistance, and causes distress. Obsessions also have a personal quality, whereas superstitions tend to be shared by many members of the community or family.

Distress and interference

What makes someone a candidate for the diagnosis of obsessive–compulsive disorder? The key question that needs to be asked is: Do the obsessions and/or compulsions cause him distress, or severely affect his functioning? If the problems are severe, they will undoubtedly cause much distress, and will interfere with his life. Experiencing an unwanted thought once a day on average could not conceivably cause someone any real distress, but, if it were to happen dozens of times every hour, that would be distressing. Similarly, checking all the gas taps once or twice before leaving home hardly interferes with one's life, but if one were to check, say, seven times on each occasion, then that would certainly interfere with one's normal functioning. Some patients reach clinics or hospitals only after the problem has progressed to such a degree as to have led to drastic effects on their lives. For example, a woman came for help only when her compulsions had developed to such an extent that she was spending all her waking hours cleaning the house. Another patient, a man, had resigned from his job because he became increasingly concerned with the germs that he thought would affect him through contact with others.

Sometimes the person's obsessions and compulsions are more distressing to others than to himself. Consider, for example, a man who had an obsessional concern about germs and dirt, and who carried out washing and cleaning rituals regularly. This might never have become a problem in itself, but he also began to insist that his wife and mother-in-law did the same. If they refused, he would get very angry with them. He began eventually to insist that they both washed their hands at certain times, that they kept their towels in certain places, and so on. The initial distress was thus felt not by him, but by others who were living with him.

In some, the compulsion is a minor one which does not affect one's life or functioning normally, but can be a problem in certain circumstances. A young man had the compulsion to look at any stranger a second time. If he noticed someone on the street who went past him, he would immediately turn round and look at the person in question once again. This was a harmless if peculiar compulsion, and remained so until he acquired a girlfriend. The latter noticed this behaviour and immediately inferred that he was showing an unhealthy interest in other women, despite the fact that he was looking at members of both sexes indiscriminately! The ensuing dispute very nearly caused the break-up of their relationship. It was this that brought him to a psychologist for advice; otherwise he may never have felt any need to seek help. In another case, a man was accosted by store detectives in a large supermarket. He admitted that he had acted in a way which might have given rise to suspicion: he had a compulsion to touch with one hand anything that he had touched with the other, even if he had to turn round and go back to the object to do so, and to make the hand in question free by transferring whatever he was carrying to his other hand. Until this embarrassing event, he had not realized what a spectacle he was making of himself in public places.

What can we conclude from all this? Both obsessions and compulsions are common among people in the general population, and they are not considered as problems unless they cause distress or interfere with one's life. If, however, someone has obsessions and/or compulsions that cause him distress, or seriously affect his life and activities, then he may need advice and help. It is this minority of people who get diagnosed as patients with obsessive–compulsive disorder.

THE RELATIONSHIP BETWEEN OBSESSIONS AND COMPULSIONS

Thus far, obsessions and compulsions have been discussed as separate phenomena. What about their relationship? In some of the examples of compulsions given above, a relationship between the two is clearly implied. We referred. for instance, to a young woman who had the intrusive thought (obsession) that she might go blind, whenever she saw black objects, which led to her engaging in a compulsive mental activity of visualizing objects of different colours (see p. 7). The relationship between the two events in this case is obvious: the obsession led to the compulsion. This is very common indeed; we know that, in the majority of cases of obsessive–compulsive disorder, obsessions and compulsions are related in this way. To give a common example, when someone gets the obsessional thought that he may have accidentally touched something that contaminated him, he is likely to feel a strong compulsive urge to decontaminate himself by washing his hands a certain number of times. These compulsions are sometimes described as 'neutralizing' behaviour as they serve the function of neutralizing, or putting right, the preceding obsession or its consequences.

In a minority of cases, the obsession occurs by itself—that is, without leading to a compulsion. Here is an example:

A young woman had recurrent thoughts and images of her wedding reception, which had taken place over a year ago. These thoughts mainly centred on the flower arrangements, which she felt had been unsatisfactory. The thoughts caused her discomfort, but there was no associated compulsion of any sort.

There are also cases, even fewer in number, where a compulsion takes place without a preceding obsession, as in this example:

A man had a compulsion to imagine car registration plates in a certain way. Every time he noticed a car licence number plate, he compulsively visualized the same plate with the number transformed in certain specific ways, such as squared, halved, or multiplied by two.

ELEMENTS OF AN OBSESSIVE-COMPULSIVE EXPERIENCE

One way to understand the relationship between obsessions and compulsions is to consider all the elements that may be present in an obsessive–compulsive experience. In Table 2, we have given a list of these elements.

Table 2. Elements of an obsessive–compulsive experience

Trigger	external/internal/none
Obsession	thought/image/impulse/none
Discomfort	+
Compulsive urge	+ / −
Compulsive behaviour	motor/cognitive/none
Discomfort reduction	+ /?
Fears of disaster	+ / −
Reassurance seeking	+ / −
Avoidance	+ / −
Disruption	external/internal/none

+ indicates 'present'; − indicates 'absent'

Trigger

A trigger is an event, or a cue, that sets off an obsession, a feeling or discomfort, or indeed a compulsive urge. A trigger may be external—that is, something in the environment—or internal. For example, a young woman had the obsession 'Did I stab someone?' or 'Will I stab my children?' every time she saw a knife or any other sharp object: the knife was the external trigger that provoked her obsession. Internal triggers are mental events which lead to the same result. A young man complained that, every time he remembered his deceased father, he experienced obsessions about death. The memory of the father was the internal trigger for his obsessional thoughts. Of course, as indicated in Table 2, triggers are not invariably present in all obsessive–compulsive experiences.

Obsession

Since we have discussed obsessions in some detail already, we shall not dwell on this here. Suffice it to note that there can be obsessive–compulsive experiences without an obsession as part of them, although this is uncommon. A trigger—for example, seeing the walls of a room—may lead directly to a compulsive urge—for example, to touch them in a specific order.

Discomfort

The occurrence of the obsession usually leads to a feeling of discomfort. It may also, less commonly, be generated simply by exposure to the trigger, or by the compulsive urge. For many, this feeling is best described as anxiety, but some patients report that what they feel is not anxiety, but general uneasiness, tension, or even a sense of guilt. 'Discomfort' is thus a better term to use here, as it encompasses all these emotions. Note that Table 2 states that obsessive–compulsive experiences always include discomfort; this may, however, not be so for non-clinical cases.

Compulsive urge

As noted above, this is the urge, or drive, that the person feels to carry out a particular behaviour, usually in a particular way. As Table 2 shows, not every obsessive–compulsive experience has this element.

Compulsive behaviour

We have discussed this in detail earlier, so we shall not dwell on it here. This is the behaviour, overt or covert, that results from the compulsive urge. When the term 'compulsion' is used, it usually refers to the compulsive urge and the compulsive behaviour taken together.

Discomfort reduction

When the compulsive behaviour is carried out in the required manner, the patient normally feels relieved; the discomfort caused by the obsession (and/or the trigger, and/or compulsive urge) is eliminated or reduced. In Table 2, we have included a question mark against this element of obsessive–compulsive experience because there are instances, admittedly few in number, where carrying out the compulsive behaviour does not lead to discomfort reduction. (Indeed, in a small number of cases, the discomfort may even increase.)

Fears of disaster

These are found fairly frequently: the patient feels that a certain disaster will happen, unless he wards it off by engaging in his compulsive behaviour. For example, an elderly man had the very strong fear that, if he did not check the gas taps in his house a certain number of times, the house would explode and go up in flames. The relationship between the specific disaster feared and the compulsive behaviour is, of course, not always logical. For example, a young man felt that his handwashing rituals prevented major accidents occurring to his family members.

Reassurance seeking

Many obsessive–compulsive patients resort to reassurance seeking, usually from members of their families. Often, obsessional thoughts such as 'Will I go insane?', 'Did I do it properly?', and 'Do I need to check the taps again?' lead to the patient asking for reassurance. When reassurance is received, the patient feels some relief from his discomfort. Reassurance seeking is often done repeatedly, much to the exasperation of friends and family.

Avoidance

This can be a significant feature in the clinical picture, although it is not part of the obsessive–compulsive experience itself. Usually, the avoidance behaviour concerns objects and situations that can potentially trigger the obsession or compulsion. For example, those with obsessions about dirt or germs, and associated washing or cleaning rituals, usually strive to avoid what they believe to be dirty or contaminating, and those with checking rituals may avoid situations that demand checking. A woman who had the obsessional thought that she might stab her children went to great lengths to avoid contact with knives, scissors, and other sharp objects. A young man who feared that he might catch AIDS, totally avoided certain areas of London. Sometimes, it is not places or things that are avoided, but behaviour. A patient may not wash in the morning, or at all, for several days because this behaviour requires a long and complicated ritual. An excellent example of avoidance of both objects and behaviour is as follows:

A married women in her late twenties had the obsessional thought that she had cancer. After several years of checking for cancer symptoms, she began to avoid any situation where she feared she might discover she had signs of cancer. Thus, she could not make her bed in the morning, or look at her used underwear, for fear of discovering blood stains which, to her, would be a sign of the dreaded illness. She even stopped looking at herself in the mirror, or at her own body. She began to wear blouses and jumpers with long sleeves so that she could not see her arms, and trousers so that she could not see her legs. She stopped washing herself properly, as she feared that she would discover lumps and such like on her body.

In some cases, certain numbers are avoided because the patient feels that such avoidance is needed in order to avert some disaster, usually to a loved one. An interesting illustration of this is found in the following example:

A young married woman began to avoid the number four. Her husband's birthday was on the fourth day of a month and her obsessional logic dictated that, if she did not avoid the number, she would cause some great harm to him. She went to great lengths to achieve this; for instance, she would skip the fourth page of books and magazines she was reading, would never write the number four, never eat four of anything (for example, potatoes or slices of toast), and so on. Life became impossible when this gradually extended to all numbers beginning or ending with four, multiples of four, those that were adjacent to four, and so on, at which point she sought help.

Disruption

When an obsessive–compulsive patient engages in his compulsion, he needs to carry it out precisely as he feels it ought to be done. If the behaviour is disrupted then, for many, the compulsive ritual is invalidated and needs to be restarted. For long and complicated rituals, this can be extremely time consuming and exhausting! The events that can act as disruptors vary from noise and other external disturbances to certain classes of experiences and thoughts.

A middle-aged man had recurrent, intrusive thoughts and images of past homosexual experiences. This led to feelings of guilt and distress. He had to 'cleanse his mind' with silent prayers to God uttered in a certain fixed sequence. If, during this praying, images of homosexual acts arose in his mind, then he had to restart the praying.

The need to form a safe or suitable thought before carrying out a compulsive, or other, act is common. If, as in the case described here, the action is disturbed by an unacceptable thought, the compulsive sequence has to be repeated in full.

A young man engaged in prolonged hand-washing rituals whenever he felt his hands were contaminated by dirt and germs. He would usually wash them at the kitchen sink. If, during this activity, he happened to catch a glimpse of the kitchen waste bin, which he considered to be a dirty object, he felt his washing was not effective. So he would restart the washing ritual.

OTHER KEY TERMS

There are two other key terms that are commonly used to describe aspects of obsessive–compulsive disorder which need explanation. They are 'ritual' and 'ruminations'.

What is a ritual?

A ritual is a compulsive behaviour, either overt or mental; it implies that the behaviour concerned has a rigid set pattern and a sequence of steps, with a clear-cut beginning and end. Some examples of compulsive behaviour are highly ritualized. The following example ilustrates a very elaborate compulsive ritual reported by a man in his mid-twenties. This is what he had to do when brushing his teeth and washing his face each morning:

Enter bathroom, with left foot first.
Close door with left hand, then touch door handle with right hand.
Take towel from rail and keep it on edge of bath with left hand, then touch it with right hand.
Take toothbrush from cabinet and place it on edge of wash-basin with left hand, then touch it with right hand.

Take toothpaste tube from cabinet with left hand, then touch it with right hand.

Unscrew and remove cap with left hand, then touch it with right hand.

Squeeze tube to get enough toothpaste on to brush with left hand, then touch tube with right hand.

Replace cap of tube with left hand, then touch it with right hand.

Put tube back in cabinet with left hand, then touch it with right hand.

Pick up brush with left hand, then start brushing: teeth brushed in twos, from left to right, top row first, bottom row next, outside first, inside next, each set of two eight times; then, repeat whole process with brush in right hand, then again with left hand, followed by same again with right hand.

Open taps with left hand, then touch them with right hand.

Wash brush under hot tap, held in left hand, then touch it with right hand.

Put brush back in cabinet with left hand, then touch it with right hand.

Rinse mouth, taking water with left hand, then with right hand.

Look at self in mirror first with left eye, then with right eye.

Begin to wash face, using left hand to splash water on face, then right hand.

Rub left side of face with left hand, followed by right side of face with left hand, then rub left side of face with right hand, followed by right side of face with right hand.

Apply soap to face, in the same sequence as above.

Rinse face, splashing water on face with left hand, then with right hand.

Look at self in mirror, first with left eye, then with right eye.

Close taps with left hand, then touch them with right hand.

Pick up towel with left hand, then touch it with right hand.

Dry face with towel, left side holding towel in left hand, then right side holding towel in left hand, then left side holding towel in right hand, and then right side holding towel in right hand.

Look at self in mirror, first with left eye, then with right eye.

Put towel back on rail with left hand, then touch it with right hand.

Open door with left hand, then touch handle with right hand.

Leave bathroom, with left foot first.

Most compulsive behaviour has a ritualistic quality about it, and for this reason the term 'ritual' is used by many to refer to any compulsive behaviour; in this book, the word 'ritual' is used in this broad sense. Similarly, engaging in compulsive behaviour is sometimes referred to as 'ritualizing'.

What are ruminations?

A rumination is a train of thought, unproductive and prolonged, on a particular topic or theme. Some authors and clinicians use the term 'obsessional rumination' to refer to all obsessional thoughts, but this is misleading. An example of a rumination is as follows:

A young man had complicated and time-consuming ruminations on the question: 'Is everyone basically good?'. He would ruminate on this for a long time, going over in his mind various considerations and arguments and contemplating what superficially appeared to·him to be relevant evidence. This never led to a solution or satisfactory conclusion.

How does a rumination differ from an obsession? Unlike obsessions, ruminations do not intrude into the patient's consciousness in a well defined form, or with a clearly circumscribed content. Clinically, it appears that ruminations are mental compulsive behaviour, usually preceded by an obsession. For example, the obsession 'Am I going mad?' may lead to the compulsive urge to think through the subject, which in turn leads to a muddled attempt at thinking about it; this is the rumination. Ruminations are different from other mental compulsions in that the latter consist of specific mental acts, such as saying something silently or visualizing something in a particular way (see examples on pp. 6–7). Ruminations, on the other hand, are not such well defined events; the theme or topic of a rumination is specific, but what goes into the thinking about the topic is open-ended and variable.

Many ruminations of obsessive–compulsive patients tend to concern religious, philosophical, or metaphysical subjects such as the origins of the universe, life after death, the nature of morality, and so on.

2. Relationship to other disorders

In this chapter, we shall briefly discuss the relationship between obsessive–compulsive disorder and some other psychiatric conditions.

Depression

There is a clear relationship between obsessive–compulsive disorder and depression. This can take several forms. Firstly, some people develop obsessions when they become depressed; in such cases the obsessions are essentially secondary to the depression, and usually clear up when the depression lifts. It has been observed that, among obsessions developing in the context of a depressive illness, about a half have a content of aggression of a homicidal or suicidal nature whereas, among obsessive–compulsive patients, such content is found much less often. Secondly, many obsessive–compulsive patients tend to have a past history of episodes of depression. Thirdly, some of these patients become depressed subsequent to the onset of their disorder, and may have episodes of depression. When depressed, the symptoms of obsessive–compulsive disorder tend to get worse. Recent research has also shown that, if the patient is very depressed, he may not respond well to the standard behavioural treatment of the obsessive–compulsive disorder. In such cases, the depression needs to be treated before improvement can be expected in the obsessive–compulsive symptoms.

In view of the relationship between the two disorders, a word is necessary about the features of depression. The major features are: seriously depressed mood; loss of interest or pleasure in usual activities; disturbance of appetite and sleep; severe slowing or agitation; feelings of worthlessness or extreme guilt; extensive pessimism; and suicidal ideas.

Morbid preoccupations

Morbid preoccupations are often found in depressed patients, and some-times in normal people during phases of low mood. There is some similarity and overlap between obsessions and morbid preoccupations: both consist of intrusive and repetitive ideas. However, preoccupations differ in significant ways from true obsessions in that they centre on realistic current problems or worries, and lack the nonsensical or repugnant quality of obsessions. They are rarely resisted, and the person usually recognizes them to be rational, if exaggerated.

Schizophrenia

The relationship with schizophrenia is more limited. In schizophrenia, stereotyped behaviour, which may appear like compulsive behaviour, is sometimes evident. It is also known that, in the early stages of schizophrenic illness, obsessions and compulsions occasionally may appear, but these are short-lived. Complaints of schizophrenic patients about thoughts that they wished they did not have can bear a superficial similarity to obsessions, but these are usually thoughts that they believe to have been put into their minds by external forces, human or otherwise. This feature makes these very different from obsessional thoughts, which the patient recognizes as his own.

Many years ago, some writers and clinicians held the view that obsessive–compulsive disorder and schizophrenia were closely related conditions. Some even took the view that the disorder is a defence against a schizophrenic breakdown. There is no evidence to support this view, and the belief in a connection with schizophrenia is discredited. The chances of an obsessive–compulsive patient becoming schizophrenic subsequently are no higher than those of any other person.

However, obsessive–compulsive patients sometimes do get diagnosed (or misdiagnosed) as schizophrenic. This is largely due to the superficial similarity between obsessions and the delusions (intensely held, personal, false beliefs) that schizophrenics commonly hold. Ordinarily, the two phenomena can be distinguished from each other. A schizophrenic delusion is a belief intensely held by the patient—that is, he has no insight that it is false (for example, he really believes that the enemies are sending radio waves to harm him), whereas an obsession is experienced as ego-dystonic—that is, not in keeping with one's own beliefs and thoughts—and is seen as unwanted. In other words, the obsessive–compulsive patient has insight; he knows that his obsessional belief—for example, that some disaster is about to happen to his loved ones—is really not valid. Sometimes the degree of insight fluctuates, but it is not totally absent in these patients. Although the patient acts on the belief by performing compulsive behaviour or avoiding certain things, there is the recognition, if not at the time of the behaviour then a few hours later, that it is ultimately irrational. Admittedly there are exceptions, but they are very small in number. In this minority of patients, the obsessional belief is held with some tenacity. In recent years, some writers have commented on such strongly held beliefs in obsessive–compulsive patients and described them as 'overvalued ideas'. Despite the strength of these delusion-like beliefs, many of these patients can ultimately be persuaded to concede that they may be mistaken.

Phobias

Sometimes, obsessive–compulsive disorders are confused with phobias, which are irrational and/or excessive fears. In view of their common features, this is not surprising. Phobias are characterized by anxiety, and most obsessive–compulsive patients experience a lot of anxiety. As noted earlier (see p. 1) both conditions fall within the category of anxiety disorders. In both, there is avoidance behaviour: a patient with a phobia of spiders will avoid going near them or to places where he knows spiders are to be found; an obsessive–compulsive patient with a concern about dirt will avoid all places and objects that he thinks contain dirt. It is certainly the case that some obsessive–compulsive patients have some phobic characteristics, particularly those with contamination fears and related washing and cleaning rituals.

However, the two disorders are different in some important ways. The ritualistic behaviour of the obsessive–compulsive is absent in the phobic. Many of the former may describe their feeling, when affected by an obsession or exposed to a triggering situation such as contact with dirt, not so much as 'fear' but as 'discomfort', 'uneasiness', or 'disgust'. A further important difference is the following: someone with a phobia usually can, if he successfully avoids the object or situation he is afraid of, feel safe and be unaffected by the problem in his day-to-day life. Someone with a phobia of elevators, for example, will avoid using elevators and will be able to lead a perfectly happy life as long as he is not forced to do so, and someone with a phobia of spiders can lead a normal life as long as he avoids encounters with spiders. In contrast, an obsessive–compulsive patient cannot escape from his problems as easily; even if he keeps away from things that trigger his obsessions or compulsive urges, he does not feel free. For example, a woman with this disorder may totally avoid knives, scissors, and other sharp objects which she fears she may use to attack people, but still frequently worry that she may commit these acts, or indeed even wonder whether she has actually attacked someone.

So, despite some similarities and overlap, obsessive–compulsive disorder and phobic disorder are different from each other.

Anorexia nervosa

Anorexia nervosa has been described by some writers as a form of obsessive–compulsive disorder. The single-minded determination to lose weight and the incessant preoccupation with food, weight, and body size and shape that these patients display have been given as evidence for this. Anorexics are commonly described as 'obsessed with thinness'. However, anorexia nervosa is a separate disorder, not part of an obsessive–compulsive illness, although there is some relationship between the two and a small proportion of females with obsessive–compulsive disorder have a past history of anorexia nervosa. Among anorexics, a sizeable sub-group has obsessions and/or compulsions, some of them quite marked. It appears that, in these patients, the two disorders coexist. Sometimes, the symptoms of the two disorders influence each other and get intertwined —that is, certain behaviour assumes significance in both disorders. For example, an adolescent girl had the compulsive behaviour of running up and down the stairs seven times before every meal. This had all the features of a compulsion, but it could equally be seen as an anorexic behaviour, designed to lose weight—and it certainly had that effect. She also had the compulsion to leave a quantity of her food on her plate, arranged in a certain way, unconsumed. Her explanation was that she felt compelled to do this. Although she denied that it had anything to do with eating less, the behaviour clearly contributed to maintaining a lower weight.

Patients with both anorexia and obsessive–compulsive problems report that their latter difficulties tend to get worse when they are particularly unhappy with their weight and body size. It is also known that anorexics with obsessive–compulsive symptoms tend to display more severe anorexic disorders than those who do not have such symptoms.

Bulimia nervosa

In bulimia nervosa, which is a variant of anorexia nervosa, the patient has recurrent episodes of binge eating, accompanied by self-induced vomiting and/or laxative abuse. The urge to engage in binge eating is described by some of these patients as having a compulsive quality, although the nature of the behaviour is by no means senseless. As with anorexics, some bulimics also have concomitant obsessive-compulsive problems, some features of which may become closely related to the eating disorder. For example, a young woman with a history of both disorders reported that, when she binged on chocolate bars, she felt compelled to eat twenty-four bars at a time, neither more nor fewer, and the binge had to be uninterrupted. If the chocolates got 'contaminated' by the smell of another food, then the whole bingeing episode had to be restarted.

Gilles de la Tourette syndrome

This condition is characterized by multiple tics, including vocal tics which may take the form of swear words or obscenities. These tics are different from true compulsions—they are purposeless and involuntary, unlike compulsions. Nor can they be easily delayed, reshaped or substituted, again unlike compulsions. Another difference is that the treatment methods that are successful with obsessive–compulsive disorder are of little use with Tourette patients.

It has been reported that some patients with this syndrome also have obsessive–compulsive symptoms, particularly the younger patients. Family members of Tourette patients have also been reported in some studies to have a higher incidence of obsessive–compulsive features than the general population. Despite these apparent associations, however, patients with obsessive–compulsive disorder rarely have the Gilles de la Tourette syndrome.

Brain damage

It is known that symptoms similar to obsessions and compulsions can result from brain damage, caused by injury or neurological disease: the patient may engage in repetitive acts or express repetitive ideas. The appearance of obsessive–compulsive-type symptoms in certain organic conditions (for example encephalitis lethargica) has been recognized for many decades. These symptoms are usually accompanied by other signs of brain damage, such as deficits in memory and learning ability. Further, the repetitive acts and ideas of these patients are different from obsessions and compulsions in that they lack intellectual content and intentionality, and have a mechanical or primitive quality. Studies undertaken to investigate neurological and neuropsychological features of obsessive–compulsive patients have not produced consistent or clear-cut results. It is safe to say that there is no evidence of any brain damage in the vast majority of obsessive–compulsive patients.

OBSESSIONAL PERSONALITY

Different views have been expressed on the relationship between obsessive–compulsive disorder and obsessional personality (also called 'compulsive personality' and 'anankastic personality'). By obsessional personality, we mean a group of enduring characteristics in a person, including orderliness, meticulousness, parsimony, obstinacy, neatness, and perfectionism. According to some writers, obsessive–compulsive disorder is only an exaggerated stage or version of an obsessional personality. This is incorrect: obsessional personality traits are acceptable to the person, seldom cause distress, are rarely accompanied by a sense of compulsion, and equally rarely provoke resistance. Perhaps even more importantly, these personality traits show much greater stability than obsessive–compulsive disorder.

A related view is that the premorbid personality—that is, the personality before the onset of the disorder—of obsessive–compulsive patients is of the obsessional type. However, neither of these views is confirmed by satisfactory evidence. It is true that a proportion of obsessive–compulsive patients do have an obsessional-type personality, but many more with very different personality features also develop the disorder. Conversely, a large majority of persons with obsessional personalities never develop obsessive–compulsive disorder.

If we were to look for any single personality type that is associated with the disorder, it is perhaps best described as cautious and introverted, rather than obsessional. Even this has to be seen as only a very general observation, for there are numerous exceptions.

Compulsive personality disorder

Persons with obsessional personality features to a degree that seriously affect their life and functioning are sometimes clinically described as suffering from a compulsive personality disorder, also called 'obsessional personality disorder' or 'obsessive–compulsive personality disorder'. In these patients, the main features are long-standing personality traits such as excessive rigidity and perfectionism, undue preoccupation with details, indecisiveness, and so on, and not episodes of illness. These features are well established by early adulthood. In addition, these people tend to show a lack of, or limited ability to express, warm and tender emotions. They do not necessarily have or develop true obsessions and compulsions. In clinical practice, such patients are encountered only rarely and, when they do come for help, it is usually due to a depressive or other illness. It has been observed that this disorder is more common in males than in females.

3. Obsessive–compulsive patients

There are several common forms of obsessive–compulsive disorder. Most patients have more than one problem, but usually there are one or two that are predominant at a given time. At the time of coming for help, many also display general anxiety, low mood, frustration, and considerable overall distress.

MAIN CLINICAL TYPES

A convenient classification in terms of clinical presentation is given below:

(1) those with washing/cleaning compulsions as the major problem;

(2) those with checking compulsions as the major problem;

(3) those with other overt compulsions as the major problem;

(4) those with obsessions unaccompanied by overt compulsive behaviour;

(5) those with primary obsessional slowness.

Washers/cleaners

This is the commonest clinical presentation. Typically, the patient has obsessions about contamination by dirt or germs, or pollution from something more specific like urine, faeces, seminal fluid, animal fur, asbestos, and so on, and related washing and cleaning rituals. There is also avoidance, in an attempt to keep away from contact with dirt or other sources of contamination or pollution. The washing and cleaning can be severely excessive; in some cases this involves washing one's hands over a hundred times a day, using bottles of detergent, using hundreds of toilet papers, bathing or showering for several hours, washing and wiping table tops, chairs, and floors for much of the day, and so on. The reasons given for the washing or cleaning are varied. Often, it is for the purpose of getting rid of dirt or germs. This is linked, in some, to ensuring that a serious illness (such as cancer) is not contracted. In some cases, the cleaning is aimed at protecting others from the spread of germs. A few say that they have to engage in the washing and cleaning ritual simply to avert the great anxiety, even panic, that would occur if it was not promptly done.

The avoidance can be extensive. The patient may not touch objects that others have touched, such as door knobs and public telephones; he may refrain from using public toilets, and avoid sitting on chairs which others have sat on, or—if he did—would first cover it with a towel or cloth or sit on the edge. In severe cases, the entire world except a small area in one's home is avoided. One woman was so concerned about dirt and germs that she felt free only in her bedroom and the bathroom, which she did not allow anyone else to enter. When she went out, she wore a large coat and gloves which she immediately washed upon return- ing. Another patient felt some safety only when sitting in her exclusive chair at home; she disinfected her chair daily (see below).

There is an excess of females over males among those whose main problem is washing/cleaning.

The following is a case illustration:

A young woman had obsessions about dirt, and related compulsions. Her main concern was about excrement, both human and animal. She would wash extensively after returning from a walk even if she did not actually see, let alone step on, dirt. This was because she felt that dog dirt is spread all over the roads and pavements by rain and wind. She would leave her shoes out at the door and change into a different pair before entering the house. She totally avoided public toilets. As the problem got worse, she began to avoid going anywhere near man- holes as they indicated the presence of sewers with human excreta underneath. She would avoid parts of roads in her area where she knew there were man-holes. By the time she came for help, she had almost wholly stopped going out, had left her job as a result, and had begun to spend much of her time in bed. She had also begun to demand that her parents, with whom she lived, stop going out, as they would bring dirt into the house when they returned, and to insist that they left their shoes outside and washed their hands and feet when they returned from an outing.

Here is another example:

A married woman in her mid-thirties developed a severe and pervasive fear of contracting cancer through contact with any person, or with things that had come close to a person with the disease. She recognized that her fear was scientifically groundless but, despite this, her fear was intense. In order to reduce the chances of contracting cancer, she spent hours each day washing, cleaning, and disinfecting herself and her clothes. She did not feel safe going out, and so did not leave her house except for the most urgent of reasons. She felt more secure in one room of the house, and on one chair in particular. Her hands were red, swollen, and abraded, due to the excessive washing.

The hands of many compulsive hand-washers show clear signs of excessive washing. The repeated washing tends to dry the natural oils of the skin and frequently causes marked dryness, especially in the areas between the fingers.

Fear of dirt and germs—a patient's account

The following is a female patient's own account of her washing and cleaning compulsions. She was in her fifties, and lived on her own in an apartment.

I cannot touch anything that I think is dirty. It is mainly the toilet, but then when you come out of the toilet you bring the dirt and the germs out into other parts of the house. I always wash my hands many times before I leave the toilet. I keep my shoes and slippers outside the door of the toilet, so I can step into them as I come out. No, I would never use a public toilet, never. I nearly died when once a young man who came in to fix something used my toilet. He just came out and went on touching things, and walking about the place, as if everything was fine! I couldn't tell him to stop, but it was *so awful*. I cleaned and cleaned all over the house after he left. I used disinfectant on the things he touched, even the things he went near. I don't like people coming into my home, not even friends, any more. My bedroom I somehow keep clean. Every other part of the house is really dirty, however much I clean. The towels I have in the toilet I wash separately, never with my other things. When I feel I am dirty I wash and wash, with lots of soap, and with Dettol and what not. The whole flat smells of disinfectant. I feel fine for a while when I have washed but, when I go to the toilet again, even to pick up something or to open the window, it starts all over again. I don't think I can allow myself to be touched by anyone. I keep my gloves on when I am in shops or on the bus. All the clothes I wear for outside, I never bring into the bedroom without first washing them. If the bedroom also got dirty then I would be finished. Where could I go? That is the only clean place which I have.

The germ war of Howard Hughes

It is well known that the late American millionaire Howard Hughes had severe contamination obsessions and related rituals and avoidance behaviour, particularly in the last years of his life. Among other things, he had complicated rituals for handling objects. For example, before handing a spoon to Hughes, his attendants were required to wrap its handle in tissue paper and seal it with cellophane tape. A second piece of tissue was then wrapped over the first protective wrapping. On receiving the spoon, Hughes would use it with the handle still covered. He had even more detailed instructions on many other things, all related to his great fear of germs and contamination, and his staff had to adhere to these instructions very strictly. Typical of these were his instructions on how to remove his hearing-aid cord from the bathroom cabinet. First, six to eight Kleenex tissues had to be used for touching the door knob to open the bathroom door. Then the taps were to be opened, using the same tissues, to obtain warm water. Next, six to eight new Kleenex tissues were to be used to open the cabinet that contained the soap, and an unused bar of soap taken. The hands were then to be washed very thoroughly, making sure that they did not touch the taps or the sides of the bowl. Next, fifteen to twenty new Kleenex tissues had to be used to turn off the taps. Now the door of the cabinet that contained the hearing-aid cord was to be opened, using at least fifteen Kleenexes. Nothing inside the cabinet was to be touched in any way, except the sealed envelope which contained the cord. This was to be removed with both hands using at least fifteen Kleenexes for each hand. Only the centres of the tissues were to be allowed to come into contact with the envelope.

On those occasions when his staff had to touch him in order to wake him up, Hughes's instructions were that the chosen person should pinch his toes with eight thicknesses of Kleenex tissues, applying progressively greater pressure until he woke up.

Checkers

Those with checking compulsions form the next largest clinical group of obsessive–compulsives. Males and females are found in roughly equal numbers in this group. These patients engage in excessive checking rituals. A typical checker will repeatedly check things such as gas taps, ovens, electrical appliances and switches, door locks, windows, cupboards, drawers, cabinets, or files. Many checkers have several of these as their checking objects. The checking is associated with obsessions which take the form of doubting, such as 'Did I switch off the gas?', 'I may have left the oven on', 'The door must have been left unlocked', and so on. Checkers worry a great deal with these doubts until they check and recheck. Checking once is not enough; often it is many times (not infrequently a fixed number of times) and even then some patients may feel vaguely unhappy. The checking takes time, it can be very embarrassing if others notice it, and it can be disabling. One young woman was not able to park her car and leave it until she had checked all the switches, radio, aerial, and all doors and windows several times. She would walk round the car, looking and checking, before leaving it. Some patients drive back home from half-way to work, to check their gas taps, light switches, and door locks.

Most checkers strive to make sure that they have not left any chance of harm coming to themselves or others. Their fear is that there will be disasters if they do not ensure that whatever they are worried about is properly checked. A middle-aged plumber had to check and recheck every plumbing job he had done, however small. If he did not do this, he felt that the pipes would burst and the building would be flooded. He sometimes invented excuses to return to houses where he had done a job, in order to do his checking. In some cases, the disasters feared are remote, and not in anyway connected to the behaviour—such as air crashes involving relatives, or even earthquakes.

While many checkers are worried about things like doors and gas taps, which many people will check (though not excessively), some checkers have less easily understood concerns. A patient may check every chair for pins or sharp objects, or for pieces of glass. For example, a young man compulsively checked every garbage bag that he walked past to make sure that it contained just rubbish, and not a corpse. Another man repeatedly drove back along the way he had just gone, to check if he had knocked down a pedestrian or an animal.

The following is a case example of a checker:

A man in his late twenties was referred with extensive checking behaviour. He felt compelled to check that 'everything was right', so he would go back over almost everything he did. The most serious doubts he had were about doors, windows, and gas taps, which he checked several times before leaving the house in the morning and before retiring to bed at night. He also checked anything that he wrote several times, which delayed his work considerably. He could not put anything in an envelope or a file, drawer, or cabinet without repeatedly checking that he had written exactly the right thing. He often ripped open sealed envelopes to reread what he had written. He also checked the dates of newspapers: while reading a newspaper, he would check repeatedly that it was that day's, even if it had just been delivered to him. Some of his checking, he felt, was necessary to avoid fires, the house being burgled, the bathroom getting flooded, and so on. For the rest, he had only a vague notion that it was necessary to avoid some unspecified calamity. At the time that he came for help, he was severely affected by the problem; nothing could be left unchecked, and his work was becoming impossible.

The patients in these examples had an exaggerated sense of responsibility: they felt that it was incumbent upon them to prevent errors or disasters from taking place and, to this end, felt compelled to carry out their checking rituals. When the feeling of responsibility of such patients is transferred or suspended, the compulsive checking tends to decline or even stop altogether. So, for example, a woman who carries out repeated checks of the light switches, gas taps, and so on in her own house, is free of these compulsions when visiting the houses of others. If these people are admitted to hospital for in-patient treatment, they typically show little or no checking behaviour in the first few days. As they settle in, however, they begin to feel responsible for the security of the ward and then their checking re-emerges.

Those with other overt compulsions

There are some whose main problem consists of compulsions which do not fall into the above categories. There is no preponderance of either males or females in this heterogeneous group. Some repeat certain behaviour, such as getting dressed or undressed several times. Some have to do things in a certain way—for example, a strict sequence has to be followed in preparing a meal or setting the table. (See pp. 17–18 for an example of an elaborate ritual of this type.) Each step is rigidly predetermined in terms of its place in the sequence of behaviour. Some have touching compulsions—touching corners of a room, touching with one hand what has been touched with the other, and ensuring equal contact time for each hand are examples. Some of the behaviour appears bizarre to others, and patients may try to conceal the compulsive behaviour.

The reason that many of these patients give for doing these things is usually the same as that given by checkers: if they did not do it, some danger or harm would happen, usually to a loved one. In some it is very specific, while in others it can be a vague feeling of harm or danger. For a few patients, the compulsion is *not* a way of warding off any harm. They say they just have to do it because, if they did not, the feeling of discomfort or anxiety would be too great to bear.

Another compulsion is hoarding: the patient feels compelled to hoard or collect large numbers of generally unimportant things and discarding things is very difficult. Old newspapers and documents are not thrown away, for fear that there may be something important in them. Some patients go to great lengths to retain their extravagant collections, often filling dozens of boxes and even devoting entire rooms to this purpose. Any suggestion that these should be disposed of meets with stiff resistance. One middle-aged man who lived on his own had his entire hallway blocked with old newspapers, advertisers' notices, free news sheets, and so on. His explanation was that he could not throw them away without first checking each and every item to make sure that he did not miss anything important. Of course, he could never do this checking satisfactorily—each time he checked a newspaper he was convinced he had not done it properly—so nothing was disposed of! There are others who hoard cans of food, old clothes, and various useless items, quite unrelated to checking.

A further interesting compulsion is list-making. The patient makes lists—of things to do, things to buy, people to telephone, and so on—well beyond the bounds of reason. One young woman had to make a detailed list each morning of every single thing that she had to do during the day, including such simple routine things as having breakfast, going to the toilet, putting on shoes, and so on. When each behaviour was completed, it was crossed off the list. Items not on the list could not be performed. This behaviour was so time-consuming that she was late for everything. When her mother once took away her notebook, she began to write on the palms of her hands.

Other overt compulsions include completing things, arranging things in symmetrical order or in some other regular way, straightening things, looking at things in certain ways, or looking at particular things, colours, and so on. Another quite common variant centres on serious discomfort arising when interrupted by unwanted intrusions. For example, while making tea, one may hear the word 'death' or 'murder' on the radio, or happen to see a 'dirty' object like a waste bin, which may necessitate the whole operation being started afresh. This is repeated until a 'clear run' is achieved. The type of event that can disrupt a behaviour and necessitate a repetition is usually something to do with dirt, danger, illness, and so on, but it can also be something of personal relevance (such as hearing the name of a loved one) or a senseless triviality (for example, hearing words beginning with 'z').

A patient's account of her day

The following is a patient's own account of the form of compulsion described in this section. She was twenty years old and was in hospital for another problem at the time that she wrote this account of her day as an in-patient. As can be seen, 'number rituals' dominated her life. Her problems had started when she was nine.

During the course of the night, I get in and out of bed four times. **7 a.m.** I get out of bed for the fourth time, put my contact lenses in and take them out four times, then make my bed, folding each corner four times, straightening the blankets and tucking them in four times, arranging the pillows four times, pulling the bed away from the wall and pushing it back in place four times, folding and unfolding the extra blankets four times, straightening the top cover four times, and drawing the curtains back and forth four times. I go to the toilet, put the lid of the toilet down and lift it up again four times, wash my hands four times, and go to the lounge counting my steps in fours in my head. I look at each corner of the room four times, counting the chairs in the room four times, and go back to the dormitory counting four times. I then pick up my washbag and put it down four times, go to the washroom counting in fours, pull the curtain back and forth four times, wash each part of my body four times, clean my contact lenses four times, brush my teeth and my hair four times, and go back to the dormitory counting in fours.

8 a.m. Breakfast—I pull my chair in at the table four times, recite in my head four different prayers four times, use the pepper four times, putting it on four different places on my plate, put my knife and fork down four times during the meal, chew the food four times or in multiples of four, and use four teaspoons of coffee, stirring it in four times. I get up from the table and go to the lounge counting in fours, get up and sit down four times, say four different prayers four times, touch each corner of the chair four times. I now shower—I step in and out of the shower four times, switch the water on and off four times, wash each part of my body four times, shampoo my hair four times, rinse my hair and flannel four times, dry each part of my body four times, put my nightdress on and take it off four times. After cleaning out each drawer of my bedside locker four times, I fold up the clothes in my wardrobe four times, change the water in the flower vase four times, dry my hair with the hair-dryer while counting in fours, put my washing into the washing machine and take it out again four times, switch the machine on and off four times, and tidy the toiletries on my locker while counting in fours, picking each item up and putting it down four times. I go to the telephone counting in fours, pick up the receiver and put it down four times before dialling, look at the dial four times, and put the receiver down and pick it up four times at the end of the conversation. After going back to the washroom counting in fours, I pull the curtains back and forth four times, go to the toilet, put down the lid and lift it up four times, wash my hands and clean my contact lenses four times, blow my nose four times, and recite in my head four different prayers four times.

Noon Lunch—I pull my chair in at the table four times, look at each person at the table four times before each course, cut each piece of food into four pieces or multiples of four, chew each piece of food four times, and swallow, counting in fours. I wipe my hands on my flannel four times, then go to the lounge counting my steps in fours, sit down and stand up four times, take my slippers off and put them back on four times, touch each corner of the chair four times, look at each corner of the room four times, look at each person in the room four times.

6 p.m. Supper—I pull my chair in at the table four times, look at each person at the table four times, and use the pepper four times.

10 p.m. I queue up for medication and count each person in the queue four times, go through to the washroom counting my steps in fours, wash each part of my body four times, brush my teeth four times, blow my nose four times, and go to the toilet, putting the lid down and lifting it up four times, then washing my hands four times. I go back to the dormitory counting my steps in fours, pull back the bed cover four times, take out my contact lenses and put them back in four times, get in and out of bed four times, hang up my dressing gown four times, draw the curtains four times, take off my slippers and put them back on four times, get in and out of bed again four times, say four different prayers four times, touch each corner of the pillow four times, and turn over in bed four times.

Those with obsessions unaccompanied by overt compulsions

There is a sizeable proportion of patients whose obsessive–compulsive disorder is characterized chiefly by mental events, with no overt rituals. Some of these have distressing obsessions only, which intrude into their thinking, such as 'My husband may get cancer', 'God does not exist', 'Am I going mad?', 'Did I say something obscene?', and so on. As noted earlier, obsessions can be thoughts, images, impulses, or—often—combinations of these (see Table 2, p. 13). They occur repetitively and make the patient anxious or uncomfortable.

In some patients, these obsessions are followed by covert compulsions, or mental rituals, which are comparable to overt behavioural rituals in that they result from a strong compulsive urge and usually have the effect of bringing about some relief. Such mental compulsive rituals include silent counting, uttering prayers or certain words and phrases silently, conjuring up certain visual images, and so on. There are some patients who have mental compulsions which are not preceded by any clearly identifiable obsession but often, patients use the mental compulsion as a means of cancelling or neutralizing a preceding obsession or the harm associated with it.

In some patients, the main problem is ruminations. We noted in the previous chapter (p. 19) that ruminations may be seen as a kind of compulsive behaviour, started in response to an obsession. The patient engages in long, unproductive thinking about a topic, either of personal relevance or of a religious or philosophical nature.

Case histories

Here is an example of someone with obsessions only.

A young married woman referred herself for help with what she described as 'unwanted ideas' which were about the possibility of her going mad. She had an aunt who had been mentally ill and who spent most of her life in a large mental hospital and, for some time, she had been assailed by the obsessions 'Am I going mad?', 'Will I end up insane?', 'Will I be locked up?', and so on. Sometimes, she also experienced visual images of herself in a locked hospital cell. The thoughts, and the images to a lesser extent, made her extremely anxious and sometimes quite depressed. She reported that the thoughts came 'at least a hundred times a day'. Her husband, to whom she turned for reassurance, somehow did not understand how distressed she was by these, and tended to laugh them off, which made her feel even more helpless. She had no compulsive rituals, either overt or mental.

The following is an example of obsessions with associated mental compulsive behaviour.

A man in his early thirties had the recurrent thought that his mother was going to die, although she was in good health. He found it very difficult to dismiss the idea from his mind, and was very upset by this. He developed the compulsive ritual of silently saying 'God is kind, he won't take her away.' He had to say this three times, uninterrupted, which relieved his discomfort. This mental ritual had the effect of 'undoing' or neutralizing the original unwanted thought.

This is an example of a mental compulsive behaviour, with no associated obsession.

A young man had the unwanted compulsion of silently repeating everything other people said in conversation. This meant that he had to be very alert, as he could not afford to miss a single word. The effect of this was that often he could not keep up with conversations, as his own contributions were necessarily limited. At the time he came for help, the compulsion had also spread to what he heard on the radio and television; he often missed the general meaning of what was being said, as he was busy mechanically repeating the words that were being uttered.

Here is an example of ruminations.

A young man had ruminations on the subject of whether he had any hereditary abnormality. The episodes, which were quite frequent, usually began with the thought 'Am I genetically flawed?' which came to his mind intrusively. When this intrusion came, he would start his ruminative thinking, carefully but unproductively trying to think the matter through. This would include thoughts about his parents, grandparents, and other relatives, the evidence for their sanity or otherwise, ideas about the heritability of mental illness, what kind of tests could be done to find an answer to this question, and so on. The thinking was quite time-consuming and rather muddled. It never yielded any solution. He would in the end give up, angry or exhausted.

Mental rituals—a patient's account

The following is an account of an elaborate mental compulsive ritual, as described by a patient. The man, in his late thirties, reported having had this problem for over a year. He also had some other obsessive-compulsive problems, but these were minor ones.

The thought is that something awful is going to happen, not to me, but to my family. It happens dozens of times a day—on some days, over fifty times. It can happen at any time, but more when I am on my own. Sometimes it is an accident, sometimes a certain illness, sometimes even death; it is not always clear which. What is clear is that something terrible is going to happen. It comes into my mind sharply, all of a sudden, and when it comes I cannot get rid of it. Whatever I might be doing at the time (say, reading a book) has to stop. The thought dominates everything else. It makes me quite anxious, and very tense. I *know* that it is irrational to worry about my family simply because of a silly thought but, when the thought comes, I *do* worry. I then have to somehow put it right: I have to cancel out the thought. I don't remember how it began, but what I do now when I get this thought is to imagine certain things. It is a very fixed sequence. I have to visualize pictures of my children, my wife, my parents—who are both dead now—then pictures of the Virgin Mary and Jesus Christ, and then pictures of two other people whom I happen to know. They have to come in this order, and always the picture of my daughter Jean has to be imagined before the picture of my son Tom. When I imagine pictures of the Virgin Mary and Jesus Christ, they have to have little golden-yellow lights around them. I don't always get these images easily; in fact, it is often quite a struggle. If it goes wrong or if I am disturbed when I am visualizing these pictures, I have to start again. Most of all, even when I have imagined the whole sequence completely, if I then see something dirty like shoes or a waste bin straight afterwards, then this makes the whole thing worthless, so I have to start again. When it is done without any such mishap, I feel greatly relieved. The tension and the uneasiness all go, and I can get back to whatever I was doing. I somehow feel that I have ensured that the family will be safe, that the disaster that I feared will now not happen. Of course, this is not rational or logical, but that is how I feel at the time.

Those with primary obsessional slowness

There is a small number of patients whose problem is best described as 'primary obsessional slowness'. This condition has been identified only in recent years, and a number of cases have been reported. Most obsessive–compulsive patients are slow as a result of their ritualistic repetitive behaviour but, in this group (consisting mostly of men), the slowness is the *primary* problem; it is not secondary to any rituals. The patient may take half an hour to brush his teeth, an hour to shave, four hours to bath, and so on. The actions most affected in this way are self-care behaviour and other simple tasks of daily living although, in some, behaviour at work is also affected. In practice, such extreme slowness in self-care behaviour makes a working life virtually impossible.

In one severe case of primary obsessional slowness, the patient took up to six hours to wash and dress himself before starting the day. He felt that he had to shave each separate hair on his face and that his shoelaces had to be exactly equal in length and to be tied with a double knot in exactly the same way each day. His everyday cleaning and dressing was divided into numerous tiny compartments, and each one had to be completed correctly and in the same stereotyped fashion each day.

In primary obsessional slowness, the person rarely resists carrying out the actions in his compulsive, meticulous way. The disorder tends to develop in early adulthood and take a chronic course, leading to increasing degrees of incapacitation. The patients tend to be socially isolated.

SOME GENERAL COMMENTS

Presence of more than one problem

It was noted earlier that most obsessive–compulsive patients have more than one type of problem (see p. 27). Washing and checking often coexist, as do other rituals and obsessions. When describing a patient as a 'washer', a 'checker', and so on, what is meant is that the patient's predominant problem at the time is of such a nature. Further, a patient with one major problem at the time of referral may well have had a different major problem, or problems, in the past. Even within the same problem, the details can change with time.

The significance of numbers

We noted that many patients engage in compulsive behaviour a specific number of times. This is particularly the case with checkers and those with various other repeating compulsions, although many washers and cleaners have special numbers, too. In a good proportion of cases, the special number has some 'magical' significance. The use of numbers also helps patients to remember how far they have reached. Although some patients can explain why a particular number has become significant— for example, the number of one's brothers and sisters, one's birth order, or one's husband's birthday—others cannot. Moreover, the key number can change with time.

Avoidance as the main problem

In some cases, the main feature may be not any active compulsive action, but avoidance of something, such as a certain number or a certain colour. In an earlier section we referred to a young woman who avoided the number four in every possible way (see p. 16)—she did not have any active compulsive rituals, either overt or mental. Some patients avoid washing, checking, or changing their clothes, as the activity in question involves exhausting rituals and takes up a great deal of time.

Indecisiveness

A feature seen in many obsessive–compulsive patients is indecisiveness. This is particularly so for checkers, whose obsessions often appear in the form of doubts, and for many of those with other kinds of rituals; however, it less often applies to washers and cleaners. Having to make a decision often triggers off doubting obsessions and related checking and other compulsive behaviour in these patients. In severe cases, the difficulty in making decisions effectively renders the patient inactive— the difficulty applies not just to major decisions, but also to very trivial day-to-day matters. For example, one young woman patient found getting dressed in the morning almost impossible, as she could not decide what clothes to wear. She would put on, then take off, several dresses. Eventually, her mother had to decide each night what the woman should wear the next day and all her clothes except these were locked away at night.

4. Impact on family, work, and social life

HOW THE FAMILY IS AFFECTED

Quite often, obsessive–compulsive disorder has a significant impact on other members of the patient's family. This may happen in a number of ways. In some cases, the patient may consistently turn to a family member for reassurance, asking questions such as 'Did I do it right?', 'Do you think I am going mad?', 'Are you sure I did it?', and so on. In most cases, the relatives provide reassurance despite the tiresome nature of the repeated requests. In some cases, family members are requested to carry out some compulsive rituals on the patient's behalf. In others, the patient may demand that others in the family follow certain rules of behaviour, and get very angry if they do not comply. The use of the bathroom is a common source of disagreement and annoyance.

Some obsessive–compulsive patients dominate and rule their families in a remarkable manner. A cleaner with an obsession about dirt may prohibit family members from entering the house with their shoes on, insist on everyone washing their hands and clothes at a certain frequency, totally bar them from certain parts of the house, and impose all sorts of other restrictions. In one case, the patient allowed only a very narrow path through the main lounge, next to the wall, for family members to walk on and—to make matters worse—they had to do this without touching or brushing against the wall! They also had to keep their towels in polythene bags to avoid them coming into contact with the patient's own towels. One young mother did not let her children or husband use the bathroom or kitchen in the morning until she had properly cleaned and washed these places, which took a good deal of time. As a result of this, on many days the husband was late going to work and the children were late for school. Another married woman did not cook for the family on most days; since she had failed to clean the kitchen and the utensils satisfactorily in time, they had to eat out. A young divorced woman got married for the second time, but would not let the new husband into her house, in case he brought contamination from outside into the house.

The children of obsessive–compulsive patients, especially of female patients, are often made to undergo all sorts of restrictions. They may have cleaning and washing rituals imposed on them or have to do everything according to a fixed routine. Friends may not be allowed to visit them. When they return from school or play, they may be made to remove their outer clothes and put them into laundry bags before entering the house. One woman insisted in giving a bath to each of her children every morning, and this was done in a rigid, ritualistic manner; each child was bathed in turn, washing certain parts of the body first, other parts next, and so on, then dried with a certain number of towels. In a minority of cases, sexual contact with the spouse may be affected or even totally cease, for example on account of fear of contamination by semen.

Why do spouses, cohabitees, parents, children, and other relatives tolerate their lives being disrupted and controlled to such a degree by a patient? Many, in fact, respond to the patient's requests and demands initially with questioning or refusal, but in the end give up and begin to comply for the sake of peace. Some family members say that they comply with the wishes of the patient out of love and kindness ('She cannot help it, poor soul'). However, many relatives refuse to comply with the patient, despite quarrels and tantrums. In some families, one key member may comply while another is totally unyielding. A teenage girl always received assurance from her mother about all sorts of doubts and worries she had, but the father never gave her any kind of reassurance. Her mother also complied with numerous demands, keeping the kitchen door open in a certain way, the clock to be kept facing a particular direction, windows kept open at a certain angle, and so on. The father, however, always refused to comply. This led to the girl's problems causing a major conflict within the family.

A mother's account

The following account, given by the mother of a 17-year-old girl with severe obsessive–compulsive problems, highlights the way in which a patient with this disorder can drastically affect the family.

Jenny would get very upset if her things were touched by any of us—even accidentally . . . Her towel is kept well away from the other towels in the bathroom, her soap is kept separate, and her toilet paper is kept in a paper bag, separate. She insists on the bathroom being thoroughly cleaned by one of us before she goes in, and she spends hours in the bathroom, washing and washing.

Jenny's chair at the dining table is kept covered with a sheet and her plate, mug, and cutlery are kept separate in a drawer. She will eat with us, but not if Ken (her brother) is there. She gets worse when Ken is at home. She says it is not really him but his girlfriend Carol that upsets her. She thinks this girl somehow makes things dirty, including Ken, and that the whole house is affected. She wouldn't let Ken touch her things at all. Carol is not allowed to come into the house now. Anything sent by her is taboo. She didn't even open the Christmas present that Ken gave her, as she felt it would somehow make her dirty, as Ken had been to see Carol that day. Now Ken stays away much of the time, and doesn't bring Carol here any more. Poor girl, she is not dirty at all. We all like her, but Jenny won't let us invite her or welcome her. Carol understands and so does Ken, but he still gets very angry sometimes. Some days ago, he threatened to bring Carol home for the day. Jenny made such a scene; she said she would leave home for good. In the end, we all felt that Carol should not come . . . But it is not only Carol and things to do with her. That is the worst, but Jenny thinks most things are dirty. She hardly leaves her room now. Most things in the house she won't go near . . . She gets me to wash her clothes separately from the others and to dry them separately. You can't reason with her. She gets very upset, or very angry. Once, she made me wash the seats of the car because I had given a lift to someone. We are all sorry for her, but we just don't know what to do.

EFFECTS ON WORK AND SOCIAL LIFE

The occupational and social effects of an obsessive–compulsive disorder depend on the severity of the problem. In mild to moderate cases, patients are usually able to continue working and maintain a reasonable social life. However, in severe cases the social and occupational effects of the disorder can be incapacitating.

Many patients manage to continue working by successfully concealing their problems. It is slowness and checking, and related doubting, that is most likely to effect an obsessive–compulsive person's occupational effectiveness. Their efficiency may gradually become noticeably impaired.

Socially, if someone spends a great deal of time checking or cleaning, or engaging in other rituals, he has correspondingly less time, or indeed inclination, to engage in social activities. If the disorder is severe, many will become restricted in their social lives. Avoidance of certain places and certain behaviour (for example, hand-shaking) out of a fear of contamination, can understandably lead to a reduction of social contact. Severe fear of contamination can also lead to visitors not being invited or allowed in one's house, as they may bring in germs or dust.

SEX AND MARRIAGE

We have already described how one's family can be affected by this disorder. It can place an enormous strain on married life. The divorce and separation rate is extremely high for people affected by this disorder, among the highest of any group with psychological or psychiatric problems.

If the obsessional fear or concern centres on contamination from bodily products, it is not uncommon to find associated sexual problems. For example, a wife may demand a state of extreme cleanliness before sexual relations, and may insist on elaborate washing and cleaning after intercourse. In some, sex may be restricted to one room or part of a room, to prevent contamination. We have come across patients whose fears included contamination by seminal fluid, which led to a total inability to engage in sexual activity.

In the majority of cases, however, obsessive–compulsive disorder does not necessarily impede the patient's sex life.

5. Prevalence and related factors

Obsessive–compulsive disorder is relatively rare, but not as rare as it was once thought to be. Studies have shown that, among psychiatric out-patients, less than 1 per cent suffer from this disorder. Among in-patients the figure is higher, but certainly under 5 per cent. There are, however, problems with figures such as these, as diagnostic practices are not consistent across clinics and hospitals.

The occurrence of the disorder in the general population, rather than among the limited numbers attending clinics or hospitals, was until recently estimated to be about 0.05 per cent—that is, one out of every two thousand. More recent findings from a systematic survey in selected catchment areas in the United States suggest a much higher figure. A lifetime prevalence of 3 per cent was found in Baltimore. In other words, three out of every hundred persons interviewed had the disorder at some time in their life. The figure was 2.6 per cent in New Haven, Connecticut, and 1.9 per cent in St Louis. This study also investigated the six-month point prevalence rate—that is, how many had the disorder in the six months prior to being interviewed by the researchers. The figures were: 2.4 per cent in Baltimore, 1.4 per cent in New Haven, and 1.3 per cent in St Louis. A similar investigation carried out in Edmonton, Canada, showed a lifetime prevalence of 3 per cent and a six-month point preval-ence of 1.6 per cent. Some authorities have argued that these figures err on the side of over-estimation but even allowing for this, these data show that obsessive–compulsive disorder is much more common in the general population than had been suspected.

It must also be remembered that many persons have obsessions and/or compulsions that do not cause sufficient distress or interference with their lives to warrant regarding them as cases of obsessive–compulsive disorder. Even among those whose problems do amount to clinical disorder, there is undoubtedly a proportion who never seek help; in fact, some positively conceal their problems. Seen in this light, the relatively high figures in the North American studies are not entirely surprising.

SEX AND AGE

There is no clear preponderance of either males or females among these patients. There are, however, some sex differences in some of the clinical groups within the disorder, which have already been mentioned (see pp. 27–38).

The onset of obsessive–compulsive disorder is usually in adolescence or early adulthood: most cases emerge before the age of 25. In one large series of patients seen in a London hospital, in 92 per cent of the cases the disorder began between the ages of 10 and 40. The onset tends to be earlier in males than in females. It is rare for someone to develop the disorder for the first time after the age of 45. By the age of 30, nearly three-quarters of all identified cases have been diagnosed. A considerable time may lapse before the affected person comes to a clinic or hospital, although this is less so now than before. The problem is more readily recognized than it was two or three decades ago.

MARRIAGE, FAMILY, SOCIAL CLASS, AND EDUCATION

Many studies show that a high proportion of adult obsessive–compulsive patients are not married and that there is a greater tendency for male patients to be single than female patients. These patients tend to get married at a later age than most, including other psychiatric patients. There is also evidence that these patients have fewer children.

It used to be widely believed by clinicians that obsessive–compulsive disorder is more common among those in higher social classes and with a higher educational background. This is probably still the case if we look at those who come to hospitals and clinics and get diagnosed as suffering from this disorder, but whether there is a true difference in terms of these factors is more doubtful. The American catchment area study referred to above did not show a higher prevalence of the disorder among college graduates when compared to others.

COURSE OF THE DISORDER

In roughly half of all cases, the problems begin and develop gradually. Among those with a less gradual onset, there is a preponderance of washers and cleaners over checkers. Generally, the course of the disorder shows some fluctuation. There may be periods when the problem is clearly present and active, followed by relatively good periods. These relatively good periods are, however, not fully symptom-free in most cases. In some, perhaps about half, there is steady worsening of the disorder. We have already noted (see p. 20) that the problems get worse with depression. Also, when the person is under stress, the chances of obsessions and compulsions reappearing, or getting worse, are greater.

FACTORS THAT CONTRIBUTE TO OBSESSIVE-COMPULSIVE DISORDER

It is difficult to give a definitive account of the factors that contribute to the origins of the disorder, as the information we have is too limited. Data from patients is mostly retrospective, and can be insufficiently accurate.

Precipitating events and stresses

Even in cases where a specific time of onset can be traced, a clear single precipitating event is not always found. However, among those where there is a single event preceding the disorder, the onset can be sudden and dramatic—onset within a matter of days or even hours of a precipitating event is not unknown. In one case, a man developed severe obsessive–compulsive problems related to fear of illness immediately after undergoing surgery for the removal of a non-malignant growth. In another, a young woman who was brutally sexually assaulted while on holiday abroad found herself thoroughly and repeatedly cleaning herself and throwing away the things she had with her at the time, almost immediately afterwards. This rapidly developed into full-blown contamination fears and extensive washing and cleaning rituals.

Such cases of clear and dramatic onset linked to a severely traumatic personal experience are not very common. On the other hand, stressful experiences of various sorts in the period of time preceding a more gradual onset of the disorder are frequently reported. These include overwork, pregnancy and childbirth, problems in marriage or sex life, illness, and death or illness of a close relative. In a significant minority of cases, the onset of obsessive–compulsive disorder is preceded by an episode of depression.

There are no known links between the nature of onset and outcome, or between the type of precipitating event and outcome.

Parental influence

Are there parental influences? If a child grows up in a household where one of the parents is severely affected by obsessive–compulsive disorder, is it likely that he will also develop the same problem? Many children briefly display comparable behaviour, but very few indeed ever develop obsessive–compulsive disorder. Children of an affected parent rarely develop lasting, specific compulsive behaviour. If anything, they are more likely to develop overdependence and timidity.

Heredity

What about genetic factors—is the disorder inherited? The kind of studies that are needed to provide answers to this question with any certainty do not exist. Of the available twin studies, comparing the occurrence of the disorder in pairs of monozygotic (identical) twins with the occurrence in dizygotic (non-identical) twins, some appear to suggest a higher rate of concordance (that is, both twins in a pair having the disorder) for identical pairs, while others have reported different findings. The same applies to studies of family members. A recently published study in London which compared the first-degree relatives (father, mother, brother, sister, son, daughter) of fifty obsessive–compulsive patients with those of a matched group who did not have the disorder, showed that the former group had a higher rate of lifetime psychiatric problems. That is, the relatives of the obsessive–compulsive patients had more psychiatric disorders in general at some time in their life, than did the relatives of the control group. However, there was no greater incidence of obsessive–compulsive disorder itself found among them.

Taken together, the available studies suggest that there is a genetic contribution, but that this does not make someone develop obsessive–compulsive disorder specifically. What appears to be inherited is a general emotional oversensitivity, or a neurotic tendency, which can predispose one to the development of some form of anxiety disorder.

CULTURE AND OBSESSIVE-COMPULSIVE DISORDER

Obsessive–compulsive disorder is found in different parts of the world, and in different cultural settings. Descriptions are available for most Western cultures, as well as India, Hong Kong, Taiwan, Egypt, and Sri Lanka, among others. The similarities of the obsessions and compulsions found in diverse countries are remarkable; the features reported in a large series of obsessive–compulsive patients in India were not very different from those found in studies in the United Kingdom or the United States.

A very early Buddhist text has an interesting account of a monk at the time of the Buddha (over twenty-five centuries ago), who engaged in what can only be described as compulsive behaviour. It is reported that the monk, called Sammunjani, spent most of his time sweeping the monastery with a broom and that this activity took priority over everything else. The Japanese Zen master Hakuin (1685–1768), who was a major figure in the history of Zen Buddhism, is described as having suffered from severe obsessive–compulsive problems as a young man. The main feature of this appears to have been obsessional thoughts in the form of doubts. This period in the life of Hakuin, who was a major religious leader in the Far East, bears interesting comparison with one stage of the life of an even more influential religious leader in the West, Martin Luther. Luther (1483–1546) is reported to have been tormented by recurrent and severe doubts and intrusive blasphemous thoughts. At this time he had, for example, doubting thoughts that he might have carried out all sorts of acts that were sinful. He also had recurrent doubts as to whether he had confessed fully and properly.

Similar unwanted intrusive thoughts of a blasphemous nature also affected John Bunyan (1628–88), the author of *Pilgrim's Progress*. He gave a vivid account of these in his autobiographical book *Grace abounding to the chief of sinners*. One of his great fears was that, instead of words of praise for God, he might utter terrible and blasphemous things. He had to resist this with great effort, and was very distressed by these unwanted thoughts. In a particularly informative passage, Bunyan describes one of his unwanted thoughts in these words:

But it was neither my dislike of the thought, nor yet any desire and endeavour to resist it, that at the least did shake or abate the continuation or force and strength thereof; for it did always in almost whatever I thought, intermix itself with, in such sort that I could neither eat my food, stoop for a pin, chop a stick, or cast mine eye to look on this or that, but still the temptation would come, *Sell Christ for this, or Sell Christ for that; Sell Him, Sell Him.*

The phenomena of obsessions and compulsions are not confined to one culture or one period of time. The basic features are essentially the same across diverse cultural backgrounds and eras.

OBSESSIONS AND COMPULSIONS IN CHILDHOOD

Many children go through phases that are marked by obsessions and/or compulsions. Compulsive behaviour such as touching things and rigid bed-time rituals, and obsession-like thoughts about various subjects, are common. These usually disappear after a time. True obsessive-compulsive disorder is rare in children.

In those children and adolescents who do have the disorder, the characteristics are very much the same as those in adults. The vast majority have both obsessions and compulsions. Cleaning and washing rituals with associated contamination obsessions are the commonest clinical presentation. Obsessions about danger, harm, death, and so on, and compulsions like checking, arranging, touching, and body movements are also found. Associated depression is found in a significant minority. A clear difference from adults is that primary obsessional slowness does not seem to occur among children.

In many cases, the child's family, usually the parents, are involved. The child may get his parents to do certain things in certain ways—for example, arrange furniture in a certain order, or repeat whatever they say—and generally to comply with his demands. Most parents comply, rather than provoke anger and tantrums in the child. One adolescent girl had ritualistic behaviour which governed many of her daily activities. At meal times, she insisted on carrying out a highly ritualized dialogue with her mother, which could take up to an hour. The mother had to answer a series of questions, and give a series of reassurances, most of which had to be repeated several times if the girl did not 'feel right'. The mother went along with these demands because, if she did not, the girl would be very upset and refuse to eat. There were similar joint rituals at bed time.

In some cases, the child conceals the problem from the family and it is detected only indirectly. An adolescent boy's obsessive–compulsive disorder came to light only after the toilet was blocked several times; he had been using vast amounts of toilet paper to clean himself in the lavatory.

Very occasionally, the disorder begins at a very early age, in some cases before the age of five. In a major American study, a case was reported in which the age of onset was three years. Boys tend to develop the disorder, on average, somewhat earlier than girls. There is also an overall preponderance of males over females among child and adolescent obsessive–compulsives. It is worth noting that a minority of adult obsessive–compulsive patients report that their problems began when they were quite young. So, it is possible that mild cases of obsessive–compulsive disorder in childhood and adolescence go undetected and untreated. Thus, the true prevalence of the disorder in childhood may be not as low as generally assumed.

The prevalence of obsessive–compulsive disorder among the parents of children with this disorder is not any higher than among the parents of other children.

The obsessions and compulsions of children need to be distinguished from autistic behaviour. Autistic children show behaviour which may appear similar to the compulsive behaviour seen in obsessive–compulsive disorder, but autistic behaviour lacks the subjective qualities of true obsessions and compulsions: there is little evidence of subjective resistance, unwantedness, senselessness, or unacceptability.

6. Theories and explanations

Different theories have been put forward in attempts to explain obsessive-compulsive disorder. It is not possible, in a short book like this, to attempt a full discussion of these theories. What we shall do in this chapter, instead, is to take a brief look at some of them.

THE PSYCHOANALYTIC VIEW

Historically, the oldest and the best known theoretical account is the psychoanalytic one. Psychoanalysis is the treatment technique for neurotic disorders that was developed by Sigmund Freud, and the assumptions underlying it are referred to as 'psychoanalytic theory'. There are many versions of the psychoanalytic theory of obsessive–compulsive disorder. Broadly, however, these views can be summarized as follows.

Obsessions and compulsions are symptoms of some deeper problem in the person's unconscious mind. Certain memories, desires, and conflicts are kept out of consciousness, or repressed, because they would otherwise cause anxiety. These repressed elements may later manifest themselves as neurotic symptoms. Fixation (or 'getting stuck') at a particular stage of development, caused by various factors during one's formative years, determines the nature of the neurotic symptoms that appear in this way in later life. Obsessive–compulsive disorder is linked in this way to the stage of development which is called, in this theory, the 'anal–sadistic stage', in which toilet training is a major feature. Anger and aggression are also associated with this stage of the child's development. Certain experiences during this phase, including desires, impulses, conflicts, and frustrations, can make one vulnerable to obsessive–compulsive disorder, and to obsessive–compulsive personality features, in later years. The compulsive acts, obsessional thoughts, and so on are seen as defensive reactions which suppress the real, hidden anxieties.

Interesting though it is, the psychoanalytic theory has little evidence to support it. It is also one of those theories that cannot easily be tested.

THE LEARNING VIEW

The other main psychological theory that attempts to explain obsessive–compulsive disorder is the learning view. This considers that neurotic disorders, and many other behavioural problems, are acquired or learned. An individual may learn, through association with a painful or terrifying experience, to become anxious about certain things which are really harmless. He may also learn that certain behaviour reduces anxiety, and this then becomes strengthened. In this case, the compulsive behaviour, because it reduces anxiety, becomes established and strengthened; the person thus engages in this behaviour as a habitual way of reducing or preventing anxiety.

There is evidence that, in most cases, the carrying out of the compulsive behaviour indeed reduces anxiety or discomfort. The discomfort coming from one's own obsessions, or from various events and objects around one, is generally reduced by the performance of the rituals. So, the compulsive behaviour is maintained because it is an effective way of reducing discomfort.

Another piece of evidence that gives some support to the learning view comes from animal studies. In certain experimental settings, animals placed in aversive or painful situations are seen to engage in previously learned anxiety-reducing behaviour in a stereotyped, repetitive way, even though this behaviour does not lead to any relief or escape from the current situation. This suggests that, in stressful situations, previously useful anxiety-reducing behaviour may be rigidly resorted to even though it has no logical relation to the present stress. The seemingly senseless ritualistic behaviour of some obsessive–compulsive patients may be seen as a similar phenomenon.

However, the learning account too has difficulty in providing a comprehensive explanation of these problems. As we noted earlier (p. 46), many patients with obsessive–compulsive disorder do not recall any initial painful experience or experiences as the starting point of their problems; that is, there is often no clear direct learning experience. Also, the theory gives no explanation as to why only certain kinds of things— for example, dirt, germs, and so on—and not others commonly become the subject of concern and lead to obsessions and compulsions. It also fails to explain the origin of the obsessions themselves, particularly those that are senseless—for example, order, patterns, symmetry, and so on—and those, though meaningful, that have no relevance to the person's history or present life.

Thus, while the learning theory view is satisfactory in some ways, it does not provide a full explanation of obsessive–compulsive disorder.

BIOLOGICAL CAUSATION

Within the past few years, it has been suggested by several authors that obsessive–compulsive disorder is caused by a biological disturbance. The biological theory proposes that the disorder is caused by a biochemical imbalance in the brain—in particular, it is claimed that obsessive–compulsive disorder arises due to an inadequate supply of serotonin. (Serotonin is a neurotransmitter—that is, a chemical substance which carries messages between cells in the brain. It is known that serotonin plays an important part in brain functioning.) This theory originally emerged from the finding that an antidepressive drug, clomipramine, which blocks the natural loss of serotonin, can produce therapeutic effects in these patients.

The biological theory has gained some support, but has also been criticized. Therapeutic effects of equal or greater magnitude than those produced by clomipramine or similar drugs have been achieved through purely psychological treatment methods—when the serotonin level is ignored. There is no evidence that people suffering from obsessive–compulsive disorder have serotonin levels that differ from those of people suffering from other comparable psychological disorders, especially other anxiety disorders, or levels that differ from people free of any such disorder. Further, there is no relationship between the amount of clomipramine absorbed and the degree of therapeutic change. Even with high doses of the drug, and hence high levels of serotonin, relatively few patients are free of obsessive–compulsive symptoms and some patients simply do not improve, even with high doses of serotonin-bolstering drugs such as clomipramine. It has also been found that the patient's initial response to clomipramine does not provide a good basis for predicting the longer term effects of this medication.

Another criticism of the biological theory is that the attempt to decide the cause of a disorder from a therapeutic effect is risky. For example, the fact that aspirin relieves a headache tells us little about the cause of the headache, and it certainly does not tell us that the headache occurred because the person was short of aspirin. The fact that clomipramine often reduces obsessive–compulsive symptoms does not mean that the disorder was caused by a shortage of clomipramine, or of the serotonin which it bolsters.

A great deal of research is being carried out at present on this issue. No doubt within a few years a good deal of new light will be shed by these studies on the biological theory. The evidence supporting the theory is, at the moment, not persuasive.

OTHER APPROACHES

Some writers have offered the view that obsessive–compulsive patients' problems are due to a cognitive defect—that is, a defect in their thinking, or thinking style. The well known difficulty of many obsessive–compulsive patients in making decisions is often cited as evidence of this. There are also some experimental results which show certain thinking patterns in most of these patients. However, the available evidence is far too weak to give support to the view that a cognitive defect or a particular cognitive style is the explanation of this disorder. Much more and far stronger evidence is needed before this can be properly evaluated, let alone accepted, as a valid explanation.

CONCLUSIONS

There is, then, no satisfactory theory that can account for obsessive–compulsive disorder. It is possible that different aspects of the problem need different explanations. Of the currently available theories, the learning view has the most supporting evidence, although this is largely restricted to the explanation of why compulsive behaviour persists. It appears, from the available data, that many factors are involved in the genesis and persistence of this disorder. As noted previously (see pp. 47–8), genetic and family factors may make it more likely that someone develops these problems. It is also clear that stressful experiences have some part, probably a very important one, to play. There is substantial evidence that stressful emotional experiences can lead to recurrent intrusive thoughts and images in people. It has been suggested that when a traumatic or stressful experience is not fully emotionally processed—that is, resolved or absorbed—it may leave residual effects that manifest themselves as various symptoms. In this way, recurrent intrusions which are normally short-lived may become chronic and persistent in some people. Perhaps this is how obsessions get established in the first place. We believe that this is a plausible account, though it needs to be properly tested before it is accepted as a valid explanation.

However, the lack of an accepted explanation does not mean that we are in a helpless position with regard to the treatment of this disorder—as with many other problems, the development of effective treatment techniques for obsessive-compulsive disorder has far outpaced the development of explanations for why and how it occurs in certain people.

7. Treatment

Most obsessive-compulsive patients can now be successfully treated, in contrast to the situation even as recently as the 1960s, when there was almost a resigned acceptance that little could be done to help them.

BEHAVIOUR THERAPY

This change has been brought about mainly by the development of behaviour therapy. Obsessive-compulsive disorder is now considered to be a good candidate for treatment using this approach, with good results.

What is behaviour therapy?

Behaviour therapy, also called 'behaviour modification' or 'behavioural psychotherapy', refers to the use of learning theory in the treatment of psychological disorders. Learning theory is the body of knowledge and ideas that psychologists have developed on the basis of hundreds of studies of how changes take place in human and animal behaviour. The use of this knowledge, and techniques based on it, for human behavioural problems was always considered possible, and several people in the early part of this century reported such use. However, it was only in the 1950s that it developed into a formalized treatment approach. This was largely due to the work of the South African psychiatrist Joseph Wolpe, who later practised in Temple University, Philadelphia. The work of Hans Eysenck in London contributed greatly to the development and acceptance of behaviour therapy as a major approach to certain psychological problems, which views many behavioural problems as learned. They are seen as cases of faulty—or maladaptive—learning, or as cases of failure to learn. In either case, it should be possible to correct matters by applying the principles of learning: the faulty learning can be undone, and new learning can be promoted. Therefore, behaviour therapy concentrates on the problem behaviour itself. It does not assume, as the psychoanalytic approach does, that the difficulty is only a symptom of a deeper, unconscious problem. Rather than attempting to unravel an assumed root cause, behaviour therapists work directly on the problem behaviour. They concentrate more on the problem as it is now, and what factors are currently associated with it, rather than its past history. Of course, therapists need to know from the patient when the problem started, how it developed, and so on, but the main focus is on the problem as it is now and the therapist's efforts are geared towards modifying this problem.

The efficacy of behaviour therapy for a range of psychological disorders is well established. For many of these, it is now considered by many practising clinicians as the treatment of choice. The early criticism that if a problem is treated directly by behaviour therapy, without going into its 'unconscious roots', it will later lead to other symptoms, has been shown to be unfounded—there is no evidence that such symptom substitution takes place.

Cognitive behaviour therapy

In recent years, the scope of behaviour therapy has been expanded to include aspects of what is known as 'cognitive therapy'. Cognitions are thoughts, ideas, beliefs, and attitudes. Cognitive therapists focus their treatment on the elicitation of the patient's cognitions that are relevant to his problems and on helping him to modify them. The most impressive work by cognitive therapists so far has been in the treatment of depression and panic. Depressed patients often have very negative thoughts such as 'I am a worthless person.', 'There is no point in my life.', and so on. Attempts are made to modify these using a variety of techniques, including challenging them, showing evidence to the contrary, and setting up situations where they are disconfirmed.

While the use of cognitive therapy is well established in depression, these principles and techniques are beginning to be used for other disorders as well, notably panic disorder. Many incorporate these within a behaviour therapy framework, and some use the term 'cognitive behaviour therapy' to characterize this approach. In this book, while we retain the original term 'behaviour therapy', we certainly recognize the value of these cognitive elements within this approach.

In the case of obsessive–compulsive disorder, there is a clear, if limited, role for cognitive therapy techniques—that is, to prepare the ground for the implementation of behaviour therapy, and to help prevent a return of the problem once treatment is over. A clear example of the value of cognitive therapy in this way can be seen in the treatment of a typical compulsive checker. Most such patients have an excessive sense of responsibility. The patient believes that he is responsible for the safety and well-being of a whole range of people; hence the excessive, repetitive checking of gas taps, electrical switches, and so on. The identification of this exaggerated sense of responsibility and a consideration of its irrationality and untoward consequences, can be a most useful preliminary step in the treatment of such a person. This kind of cognitive work often plays an important part in therapy for obsessive–compulsive patients.

Cognitive behaviour therapy is in the process of development and one can reasonably anticipate important advances in the near future.

EXPOSURE AND RESPONSE PREVENTION FOR THOSE WITH OVERT RITUALS

The systematic application of behaviour therapy to obsessive–compulsive disorder goes back to the mid-sixties when a psychologist in London, Victor Meyer, began to treat patients who had compulsive rituals with what he called 'apotrepic therapy'. It consisted of two elements: placing the patient in real-life situations which made him feel anxiety or discomfort and triggered off his compulsive urges (*in vivo* exposure); and preventing the patient from carrying out his compulsive behaviour (response prevention). This combination of *in vivo*—or real life—exposure plus response prevention is now a very well established technique for treating patients with overt compulsive behaviour. Research in Britain, the United States, and the Netherlands has further developed and refined this treatment and provided convincing evidence of its efficacy. It is the treatment of choice for these patients today.

It should be noted that some authors and clinicians refer to the therapy package as 'flooding and response prevention', because the exposure carried out in this treatment is usually intense and prolonged, hence the word 'flooding'. This will become clear in later paragraphs, when the details of such therapy are described. In this book, we shall use the more descriptive term 'exposure'.

Rationale

Before describing the details of this form of treatment, we can briefly note the rationale behind it. Typically, an obsessive–compulsive patient with overt behavioural rituals experiences discomfort and a strong urge to ritualize, when provoked by the occurrence of the obsession, or by exposure to the trigger stimulus or situation. When the patient engages in the compulsive behaviour (say, hand washing) the level of discomfort goes down. But what would happen if the discomfort and the urge to engage in the compulsive behaviour were provoked but the patient was then prevented from carrying out the compulsion? Several studies have shown that, in this situation, the level of discomfort and the strength of compulsive urge still go down, but much more slowly. When this is done in repeated sessions, day after day, there is a cumulative effect leading to the patient feeling progressively lower levels of discomfort and weaker urges to engage in the compulsive behaviour. Also, the urges and discomfort decline progressively more quickly as treatment progresses.

The role of modelling

In the practice of therapy, modelling is often added as a third element in the treatment package. This refers to the therapist carrying out the action that he instructs the patient to do—touching door handles, for example—in the presence of the patient, by way of demonstration. He does this in a calm and controlled way, with no sign of discomfort. He also models coping with this exposure, without needing to wash and clean. Modelling facilitates therapy, and often is needed to assist a fearful patient to carry out certain behaviour needed in treatment. It is, however, not an essential ingredient. The essentials are exposure and response prevention.

Imaginal exposure

In some cases, imaginal exposure, also called 'exposure in fantasy', is used. This may be done for situations to which it is not practical to expose the patient in real life, and also as an initial step to prepare the patient for *in vivo* exposure to a situation. Some research in the United States suggests that, for patients who fear that disasters may occur in the future if they do not engage in their compulsions, imaginal exposure to these disasters may be a useful additional element in therapy. A patient may be asked, for example, to imagine, very vividly and clearly, a bloody accident or air-crash involving a loved one—the disaster he fears. Such imaginal exposure is claimed to improve the long-term results of therapy, when used in addition to *in vivo* exposure and response prevention.

Therapy in practice

How is the treatment done? It is important to stress that different therapists will set about their task in different ways, although the same principles are involved. So, the account given below should not be taken as a summary of what all therapists do, but rather as an example that highlights the general principles and issues.

In the assessment (see below, pp. 80–8) the therapist obtains detailed information from the patient about the full range of his difficulties. At this stage, the patient's beliefs and attitudes relevant to the problem are explored and discussed. The rationale of the treatment is also discussed in detail. The therapist and the patient then discuss the priorities and decide which compulsion, or set of compulsions, will be treated first. For each selected target, the therapist asks the patient for a full account of the objects or situations that trigger the obsession and/or lead to his compulsive rituals. A list is constructed indicating how difficult these triggers or cues are for the patient to face. This is usually done by asking the patient to give a rating of discomfort that he estimates he will experience in each of these situations, usually on a 0–100 scale (where 0 means 'no anxiety or discomfort' and 100 means 'extremely severe anxiety or discomfort'). An example of such a list, or hierarchy, is given in Table 3. Similar ratings may also be obtained for the strength of the compulsive urge, with 0 indicating 'no urge' and 100 indicating 'extremely high, irresistible urge'.

The therapist and the patient then agree on where in this list, or hierarchy, exposure should begin. Ideally, it is best to tackle a high point, even the highest, early on, but in practice many patients are reluctant to agree to this. The starting point is often the highest item that the patient is willing to try despite his discomfort, provided it is not too low in terms of discomfort and compulsive urge. He is then exposed to this in an active, even exaggerated, way. Exposure to several related items may be tackled together. For example, if the concern is with dirt and germs on the floor, door handles, and so on, the patient is made to touch very thoroughly, with the therapist usually first modelling the actions, several door handles, the floor, the rim of the dust bin, and so on. The 'contam-

Table 3. An example of a hierarchy of problem situations of an obsessive–compulsive patient

Items	Discomfort 0–100	Compulsive urge[1] 0–100
Using a public toilet	100	100
Touching the inside of the kitchen waste bin	95	90
Picking up something from the floor of the toilet at home	80	85
Touching the toilet seat at home	75	70
Touching the outside of the kitchen waste bin	70	75
Picking up something from the kitchen floor	70	70
Shaking hands with a stranger	65	55
Using a public telephone	60	50
Touching door handles in a public place	55	45
Bumping into a stranger	55	50
Touching money given by a cashier in a supermarket	50	35

[1] The strength of the urge to engage in strenuous handwashing after the activity concerned.

ination' may then be spread to his arms and clothes by getting him to rub his hands on them. This exposure is followed by a period of response prevention. The patient refrains from washing or engaging in any other cleaning ritual. The therapist usually stays with him during this time. It is extremely rare for a patient to need to be actually physically restrained from engaging in the compulsive behaviour. In fact, most therapists agree that this should never be done, since the patient needs to be sufficiently motivated to comply with the response prevention instructions —if this is not the case, no amount of coercive work will be useful.

The therapist will be sympathetic about the patient's discomfort, and help to make it easier for him—for example, by distraction, conversation, and so on. The response prevention period with the therapist may last for two hours or so; by this time, the patient's discomfort arising from the exposure, and the related compulsive urge, will normally have come down considerably. If they are still high, the session will be continued until there is a significant reduction of these, particularly of discomfort. The patient is instructed not to engage in the ritual even after this time period. Normal washing is allowed, as needed for reasons of hygiene, but the patient must not ritualize or exceed the set limit. After normal washing, the patient may be instructed to recontaminate himself so that the exposure continues. In some programmes there is strict round-the-clock supervision but with the majority of patients, this is not usually necessary.

Another important requirement in this therapy is not to give reassurance. The patient may ask for reassurance from the therapist or, at home, from a family member. These requests are not complied with. Family members are instructed not to give any reassurance. If, for example, the patient asks 'Are you sure nothing will happen?' or 'Are you sure it is all right?', the family is asked to respond with something like 'We agreed not to talk about that, didn't we?' or 'Remember, your therapist told me not to answer such questions.'.

It sometimes happens that a patient, out of his great unease during the response prevention period, engages in brief, unnoticeable rituals, or even mental rituals as a temporary substitute for the real ones. These possibilities are usually discussed by the therapist with the patient before the programme begins, so the patient will do his best not to resort to such means, which can only frustrate the therapy. Equally, in the exposure part of the treatment, a patient may touch the contaminating object very briefly and/or just with the tips of his fingers or the back of his hand. This does not help, as the resultant discomfort and the compulsive urge may then be not very high. Again, the therapist usually explains that proper exposure is needed, and makes sure that this happens.

It is possible to expose the patient continuously, for hours and even days, to the discomfort-arousing stimuli. For example, if animal fur is the major source of discomfort, the patient may be made to carry a small packet of dog hair in his pocket all the time. A patient with obsessions about the colour black may be instructed to wear black underwear and to sleep on a pillow which has a black pillowcase.

Sessions are held quite frequently in the early stages of treatment. Numerous stimuli or situations are used from the hierarchy, or from several hierarchies. The patient is told at the outset about the need for a good deal of time to be set apart for therapy. Because of the time factor, a therapist may also use others as cotherapists, or helping therapists, who need to be fully familiar with the patient's problems and the details of the treatment programme.

It is preferable for the patient not to be taking anxiolytic drugs at the time of treatment. Those who have been taking medication such as diazepam (for example, Valium) may be taken off it, or have the dosage reduced, because the anti-anxiety effects of the drug may impede the effects of exposure and response prevention treatment. As mentioned above (see p. 59), the rationale for this type of approach is that the anxiety or discomfort must be provoked, and then extinguished by allowing it to dissipate spontaneously. So any drug, including alcohol, that blocks or reduces the anxiety may hinder this effort.

The details of the programme always depend on the individual patient's problems and how the therapist plans to deal with them after joint discussion—no two patients are alike, and the therapist has to develop a suitable programme for each case. When the therapy is done on an out-patient basis, which happens in the vast majority of cases, a family member may be enlisted as a cotherapist who can help with supervision, or even extra sessions, at home. Patients are given specific homework sessions to supplement the work in the clinic. If an in-patient programme is used, either because of the severity of the problems or due to practical difficulties in implementing therapy on an out-patient basis, attempts will be made to carry out most of the sessions away from hospital and in the home situation as soon as practicable. A family member may be invited to participate in some of the therapy, even in hospital.

A case illustration—the treatment of a washer

Here is a case example illustrating the exposure and response prevention therapy package.

A 22-year-old male undergraduate was referred with extensive washing rituals, related to obsessions he had about being contaminated by dogs. Specifically, he feared that he might catch rabies (although he knew that the chances of this were slim) or some other infection. He engaged in repeated and time-consuming washing rituals every time he felt he was contaminated; this would happen if he passed a dog or saw dog faeces on the road, if someone who had been with a dog came near him, or if he happened to touch or brush against anything to do with dogs, like a discarded collar or lead, or a feeding bowl. He also had a great deal of avoidance behaviour. He would cross the road to avoid having to pass a dog. He began to avoid friends and others who he knew had dogs (in the end, he stopped going to classes). He would throw away any item of clothing he happened to be wearing when he went past or got anywhere near a dog. His life became very restricted as a result of this. He had no other obsessive–compulsive behaviour except some minor checking behaviour which was not causing any problems.

Initial cognitive exploration showed that the patient recognized the irrationality of his behaviour, but he did not feel confident about this. The rationale of the behavioural treatment was explained to him, which he was able to accept. He was treated with exposure and response prevention, with modelling. A list of situations which caused anxiety in him was prepared on the basis of ratings of severity given by him, on a 0–100 scale. He was willing to accept exposure to the highest four items in this list. These were: touching a dog with both hands (anxiety 100); touching a bowl from which a dog had eaten (anxiety 90); touching a piece of cloth which had come in contact with a dog (anxiety 80); and walking barefoot on the ground where dogs had previously been (anxiety 75). The exposure to the first three items involved him having to touch the item very thoroughly, and then rubbing his hands on his clothes and arms. He was not permitted to wash his hands or take a bath, nor was he permitted to change the affected clothes for a period of three hours after each session. He had two or three treatment sessions a day. He had to keep with him, all the time, a piece of cloth which had been rubbed thoroughly on a dog in his presence, even keeping this under his pillow when he slept to ensure continuous exposure.

Despite being very anxious to begin with, he co-operated well with the programme and, within a few days, was very much improved. The lower items in the original list (for example, holding the hand of someone feeding a dog, anxiety 50) did not prove to be difficult when he was later asked to do them. He began to display fewer and fewer avoidance behaviours, and began to move freely and use public transport.

This patient maintained his gains well. At one stage, several months later, when he noticed some signs of the problem returning, he in fact treated himself, as he now knew what the principles of therapy were, and quickly brought the problem under control.

Therapy for other overt rituals

Although the example above was about the treatment of washing and cleaning compulsions, the principles of exposure and response prevention are applicable to all compulsive rituals. For checking compulsions, the patient is made to engage in behaviour that provokes checking (for example, leaving the house, closing drawers, putting things into envelopes and sealing them, switching off electrical appliances, and so on), and prevented from carrying out checking. An effort is made to ensure that no reassurance is given.

A compulsive hoarder will have a treatment programme in which a set of goals are agreed with regard to the disposal of hoarded items. These will be systematically carried out, initially under supervision. For example, an early goal may be to throw away all store receipts that go back ten years or more, without checking. This will be followed by other agreed goals—for example, letters over five years old, old telephone bills and local newspapers, and so on.

Those with compulsions to do certain things in certain bizarre ways are made to engage in this behaviour in other, more normal, ways. For example, a patient who does not leave a room without touching the four walls will be taken into and made to leave rooms, but with no touching. Someone who has to have his table and wardrobe arranged in a very rigid way, will be made to disarrange the things on the table and in the wardrobe, and discouraged from putting them back in his compulsive fashion. In short, any overt compulsion can be treated by this approach.

Reduction of avoidance

All of these programmes need to have built into them the reduction of avoidance behaviour. Even after successful therapy focused on difficult target situations, a patient may still avoid many other situations, partly out of habit and partly due to residual worries. Patients are therefore encouraged to go out of their way to expose themselves to all sorts of situations which can provoke rituals, not just to those to which they have been exposed in the therapy sessions.

In cases where the major problem is compulsive avoidance, the main therapeutic strategy is to extensively expose the patient to the avoided situations or things. Let us illustrate this with two case examples.

The first is the young married woman who avoided the number four, described on p. 16. It will be recalled that she did this in her obsessional belief that, if she did not, her husband would come to some harm. This avoidance behaviour of hers extended to all areas of her life and dramatically restricted her functioning. The treatment given to her included exposing her to the number four in numerous ways, many of them continuous. She was made to do many activities four times, she had the number four painted on the walls and ceilings of her room, she carried pieces of paper with the number four written on them in her pockets and handbag, and so on. She considerably improved very quickly.

The second example is the woman who had an obsession about cancer, described on p. 16. She had extensive avoidance behaviours at the time of referral and was admitted to hospital. She avoided doing anything which she feared might lead her to discover signs of cancer. Her treatment programme consisted of getting her to engage in all the behaviour that she avoided, initially with supervision and help. For example, she was regularly made to look at herself in a full-length mirror, to wash and bath herself, to make her bed in the morning, to wash her underwear without looking away, to palpate her breasts, and so on. She had long sessions with the nurses during which she had to do these things, very thoroughly. This treatment programme led to considerable improvement within a short period of time. At five years' follow-up, she was still free of the problem, and living normally.

Results of therapy

If the therapy is carried out properly and consistently, the results of such exposure and response prevention programmes can be quite impressive. There may be initial distress, and some patients may even want to give up therapy, but, once this stage has passed, it becomes easier. The therapist needs to be supportive but firm, and to have a good relationship with the patient. A substantial amount of therapy time may be needed: dozens of sessions rather than two or three, and each needs to be long, at least initially. When the patient repeatedly experiences reductions in discomfort and in his compulsive urges despite being exposed to whatever he is worried about, his own confidence increases. The new freedom he begins to feel as his problem gradually comes under control is very rewarding. One patient said, 'I can go anywhere now. I can do so many things which I couldn't even imagine myself doing. This is wonderful.'

This freedom, paradoxically, can be a problem. If the patient has been severely affected for some time, he may have had a very limited life, socially and otherwise. The family, too, is likely to have developed a lifestyle revolving around the patient's problems and demands. The patient's improvement now gives both him and his family a good deal of freedom and free time. New activities, or restarting of old activities, are needed. In short, they have to readjust to normal life. Most therapists nowadays will make it a point to help patients and relatives by counselling them in these matters.

TREATMENT FOR THOSE WITHOUT OVERT RITUALS

The treatment of these patients is not as well developed, and therefore not as successful, as that of those with overt rituals. However, there are several techniques that are used, and many patients benefit from them.

Thought-stopping

For more than thirty years, thought-stopping has been used by therapists for treating obsessional thoughts, impulses, and images. Typically, the therapist asks the patient to sit or lie in a relaxed way, and to close his eyes. The patient is then asked to verbalize the thought. When he does this, the therapist shouts 'Stop!' quite loudly; this can be accompanied by another loud noise, like the banging of a ruler on the table. This procedure is repeated several times. In the second stage, the patient is asked simply to get the thought and to indicate to the therapist that he has got it using a prearranged signal, such as raising his index finger. At this point, the therapist interrupts the thought by shouting 'Stop!'. This, too, is repeated several times. In the next stage, it is the patient himself who will shout 'Stop!'; and, after some training in this, he will move on to the final stage, where he makes his stop command silently to himself. Some therapists recommend the addition of an extra element at this stage to interrupt the thought more effectively: it is suggested that the patient wears a rubber band on his wrist which he pulls and releases against the wrist at the same time as he silently says 'Stop!'. This mildly painful stimulus is claimed to add to the efficacy of the procedure.

Variants of thought-stopping include thought-switching or thought-substitution, where the patient is trained to dismiss the unwanted thought and to think another thought, usually a preselected pleasant one, in its place. Another variant is training in thought-control, where dismissing and re-obtaining of the thought is repeatedly done, as a way of developing voluntary control over it.

Distraction

Distraction is often a useful strategy for dealing with obsessions, which arises out of the frequently made observation that obsessional thoughts, images, and so on, are most likely to intrude into someone's mind when he is alone or unoccupied. Therefore, patients are advised to distract themselves when intense and disturbing obsessions begin to torment them. One of the most effective methods of distraction is to seek out company, start a conversation, make a telephone call, and so on. For some patients, less demanding actions such as listening to music or reading may act as a sufficient distraction but, in general, the more demanding and more active kinds of activity are most effective.

Exposure to obsession

Another approach is to get the patient to expose himself to the thought—in some ways, the opposite of thought-stopping. This is referred to as 'habituation training', as the aim of this technique is to get the patient to get used to the unwanted thought. Due to repeated and/or prolonged exposure, the thought should gradually become less and less noxious; it should, eventually, no longer arouse anxiety or discomfort, and therefore cease to be a problem. In the application of this approach, the patient is asked to get the thought and keep it focused in his mind, dwelling on it, without losing it. In this way he is exposed to the thought for prolonged periods, perhaps up to one hour. This may require some prompting by the therapist as the thought would normally tend to slip away when the patient tries to keep it in focus. An alternative and often useful way of ensuring prolonged exposure is to ask the patient to write out the thought, repeatedly, for long periods.

Recent reports suggest that the chances of effective exposure to the obsession can be considerably enhanced by the use of an audiotape. The unwanted thought is recorded in the patient's own voice, on a loop tape. The patient wears headphones connected to a small tape player. When the machine is switched on, the binaural input ensures that he hears the verbalized thought clearly and repeatedly. An added advantage of this innovation is that the exposure sessions need not be confined to the clinic.

A slightly different version of this approach is to expose the patient to the unwanted thought for periods of several minutes repeatedly, rather than for one long period, in a session. Again, this can be done effectively with the help of an audiotape and headphones.

Exposure to triggers

If the obsession is triggered by an external stimulus, exposure to the trigger may be used as an aid to help the patient to form the thought in therapy. Take, for example, a young mother who complains of the unwanted thought of harming her children, which is triggered by the sight of knives and other sharp objects. She may be exposed to these objects to promote the formation of the thought.

Also, such exposure can be used as a therapeutic technique in its own right, especially for patients who show much avoidance of the trigger(s). Repeated and prolonged exposure to the trigger makes the patient less anxious and tense in its presence, and avoidance will decrease.

Often, it is necessary to ensure that the patient is exposed to the trigger and to the obsession at the same time for relatively prolonged spells. This is in order to give the patient the chance to get used to the unwanted thought in the presence of the trigger. Once again, the audio-tape technique helps considerably to achieve this dual exposure.

Exaggeration of thoughts

Some clinicians have reported the use of what has been called a paradoxical approach in the treatment of obsessions, which is best regarded as a version of the exposure approach. The patient is asked to think the target thought not just as it normally intrudes into his consciousness, but in an exaggerated fashion. For example, if the obsession is about harm to a family member, then the patient may be asked to think or imagine the worst possible scenarios with regard to that theme, whenever the unwanted thought occurs naturally, in addition to doing so in sessions with the therapist.

Treating covert compulsions

For those with covert (or mental) compulsive rituals, the approach should in principle be like that for those with overt rituals. This would require exposure to whatever stimulus, which may be an external object or an internal one such as an obsession, which will make him want to engage in his mental rituals, followed by the prevention of the ritual. This is more easily said than done; preventing a mental compulsion is not nearly as easy as preventing an overt, motor ritual, either for the therapist or for the patient himself. In order to prevent mental rituals, the therapist and the patient must consider various possible means and use what seems best. Distraction with tasks like mental arithmetic has been found to be useful. The common thought-stopping techniques can also be used as a means of stopping the mental ritual.

The following example illustrates this.

A middle-aged woman had the mental compulsion to correct any asymmetrical figure or pattern that she saw by imagining it in perfect symmetrical form. She had to do this every time she saw an asymmetrical object, or the image of it intruded into her mind, which happened frequently and made her quite tense. She often had to work very hard at the 'correcting image', until she got it absolutely symmetrical. The treatment consisted of exposing her to various asymmetrical patterns, which she was instructed to look at carefully, and then blocking her mental compulsive behaviour with self-administered thought-stopping. Another technique used to stop the compulsion was mental arithmetic.

Thought-stopping is a blocking procedure and seems particularly suited for mental compulsions. It also can be useful for ruminations, which are a form of mental compulsion. Exposure, on the other hand, is a technique that reduces anxiety or discomfort, and is best for discomfort-arousing obsessions. It is unsuitable for mental rituals. When exposure is used for unwanted thoughts, it is important to make sure that neutralizing thoughts or other mental rituals, however brief, do not take place. The therapist will discuss this in detail with the patient, and help him in dealing with any difficulties.

Setting aside a time

A technique that has been used with some success for dealing with worry may also be used for treating ruminations. This simple technique consists of setting aside a specific time of the day for the patient to do all his ruminating. If a rumination gets started at any other time, the patient reminds himself that he has a set time to do it, and this could help him not to engage in the compulsive thinking ruminatively. For example, a 35-year-old lawyer who was tormented by repetitive doubts about a conversation he had with a client, learned to postpone the ruminations by agreeing with himself to worry about it at 10 p.m. When the agreed time arrived, the urge to recycle the troubling thought was invariably weak or absent.

This kind of delaying tactic can also be useful in dealing with covert neutralizing rituals. When an obsession occurs and the patient feels a strong urge to neutralize it with his set mental ritual, he could agree with himself that it will be done at a later time. When the set time comes, the urge to carry out the ritual is usually negligible.

The problem of images

In some cases the obsession takes the form of mental imagery (see Table 2, p. 13). When the main problem of the patient is an intrusive image, special techniques can be used. With some practice one can learn to manipulate and play about with one's mental images. In experiments, normal subjects have been shown to be able to rotate, expand, shrink, and otherwise manipulate their visual images. This facility can be improved with practice. If an obsessive–compulsive patient complains of distressing images, he may be instructed to deal with the image by modifying it in various ways. A patient whose unwanted, intrusive image was of dog faeces, was trained to shrink the image; with practice, he acquired the ability to make the image smaller and smaller, until it became just an innocuous dot. Another patient who complained of distressing images of a violent scene was trained to focus on a marginal detail of the image and 'zoom in' on this part. In this way it was possible to make this part of the image, which did not arouse discomfort, larger and larger, so that the discomfort arousing part of the image 'overflowed' from the image space. The image thus became less upsetting. Such techniques as these for manipulating one's unwanted images are effective probably because of the sense of control the patient gets in successfully doing so. After all, one of the reasons why obsessions are a problem is that they come despite one's resistance and are hard to dismiss. If, therefore, the patient achieves some control over the image, that makes it less of a problem.

Results of therapy

The results of therapy for obsessions, mental compulsive rituals, and ruminations are variable. Some patients respond satisfactorily, while others do less well. Sometimes, a therapist and a patient will try out several techniques until some improvement occurs.

In the treatment of these problems, it is important to attempt to apply the technique most suited to the particular nature of the problem of the individual patient. Until quite recently, many therapists attempted treating covert obsessive–compulsive phenomena without the fine and detailed analysis that is needed for a rational approach. For example, it appears that many patients were treated with thought-stopping, irrespective of whether their problem was a mental compulsion or a pure obsession. It is not surprising, then, that the results of the treatment of these problems have not been all that impressive. On the other hand, if therapy is based on a close and detailed analysis of the actual phenomena that a patient experiences so that each type of problem is treated with the appropriate technique or combination of techniques, the chances of success are greater.

THERAPY FOR PRIMARY OBSESSIONAL SLOWNESS

For those patients whose problem is primary obsessional slowness, a therapy involving pacing, prompting, and shaping is used. The patient's behaviour is paced, with repeated urging to speed up. Time limits are set for selected behaviour and the patient is helped to keep to these time targets. The therapist assists by prompting the patient. Some modelling may be used as well: the therapist may demonstrate, for example, how to comb one's hair in just two minutes, and get the patient to do likewise. The patient is also given feedback on how well he is doing, and praised for completing a behaviour quickly. A selected target behaviour may be 'shaped', in the sense that the time allowed for it in each session is gradually shortened.

This kind of treatment is very time-consuming and requires a great deal of input by the therapist. Some of these patients require initial hospital-based treatment and after the in-patient phase much home-based therapy is also needed. These patients improve only gradually, and may not retain their improvement unless further help is given by booster sessions. Fortunately, patients in this category are few in number.

A case illustration

An example illustrating the treatment of primary obsessional slowness is given below.

A 38-year-old man with chronic and severe obsessive–compulsive disorder was referred for treatment. The main feature of his disorder was excessive slowness— he took roughly three hours to prepare himself for work each morning. He bathed infrequently because he needed up to five hours to complete the process.

By the time he was referred for help, he was in danger of losing his job, as he was regularly quite late for work.

In the treatment programme, a wide range of self-care behaviour was dealt with. Only the management of brushing his teeth is cited here, as an example. Initially, he was advised and instructed on how to brush his teeth in a reasonable length of time. This produced a small impact, but soon a plateau was reached beyond which no improvement took place—a typical feature with these patients. Then, the patient was asked to carry out the brushing in the presence of the therapist for a few occasions; it was clear that the slowness resulted from his wish to brush each tooth in turn, in a particular sequence, and in a meticulous manner. He was then given a demonstration of brushing teeth at normal speed, and he was asked to imitate the therapist. Some improvement was obtained immediately. In the next stage of therapy he was instructed to brush his teeth on a number of occasions during which the therapist set up a speeded-up goal and provided time checks each thirty seconds. This produced further improvement, although the patient found it difficult to break the five-minute barrier, which was the agreed goal.

Following this approach in dealing with all of his problems, a significant overall improvement in bathing, washing, teeth cleaning, and dressing was achieved. He gradually learned to complete his daily self-care chores in an acceptable manner and period. The improvements ensured that he was able to retain his job.

OTHER BEHAVIOURAL TECHNIQUES

Various other behavioural treatments have also been used with obsessive-compulsive patients. One is systematic desensitization, in which the patient imagines problem situations in a graded series of steps while under relaxation. This is a common treatment for phobias. Sometimes this also includes real life exposure to situations. In this procedure, anxiety or discomfort is kept to a minimum, in contrast to the exposure-response prevention approach where discomfort is provoked.

Contingency management is an approach which manipulates the consequences of a behaviour. For example, if a patient's rituals get a lot of positive attention and sympathy, an attempt may be made to ensure that the rituals cease to produce favourable results. Instead, alternative behaviour is rewarded. Sometimes, aversive procedures are used; for example, a mild electric shock, or the use of a rubber or elastic band (see p. 67) for obsessions. On the whole, these techniques have been shown to have only a limited effect.

The use of contingency management does have an important part as an additional element in therapy, in some cases. If it is clear that the patient's obsessive–compulsive behaviour has become very rewarding to him, then the results of any exposure–response prevention programme may be attenuated by this factor. For example, a rather shy and timid young man who had severe obsessive–compulsive problems including excessive avoidance of going out was treated with standard behaviour therapy but the results were short-lived. It quickly became clear that the disabilities caused by the problems (inability to go out, wash his own clothes, to do any outdoor work, and so on) had the effect of his mother doing everything for him and waiting upon him. It was necessary to break this pattern of events through counselling sessions in which the mother was fully involved, before the young man's problems could effectively be brought under control. This is a somewhat atypical example, but the general principle that it illustrates is clear. Do the obsessive–compulsive symptoms bring any 'benefit' (such as attention, endearing words, or work being done for him) for the patient? Therapists will normally look into this in their analysis of the problems. Such an analysis that looks closely into a problem behaviour and its triggers or antecedents on the one hand, and its consequences on the other, is called 'functional analysis'. If a functional analysis shows that the symptoms do lead to such 'benefit' for the patient, some work will be undertaken to change this pattern, in addition to the main treatment techniques used.

Sometimes, these patients are taught muscle relaxation. This is a fairly simple procedure, in which one is instructed to relax all the major muscle groups in the body in a series of exercises. Some therapists would have the patient in a relaxed state for thought-stopping, although this is not seen by many as an essential ingredient. Training in relaxation can also help obsessive–compulsive patients in an indirect way; stress and tension tend to make one's obsessions and compulsions worse. Sometimes, the problem reappears after a relatively clear period of time, in the wake of stressful experiences. Therefore, if one learns to relax oneself as a means of coping with stress and of reducing tension, it can be of considerable use later.

A simple guide to relaxation is given in Appendix 1.

PROBLEMS IN THERAPY

Effects of depression

It is known that the chances of an obsessive–compulsive patient bene-fiting from behaviour therapy are reduced if he is very depressed (see

p. 20). These patients are best treated after their depression has been successfully treated by other means.

Motivation and co-operation

Some patients find the demands of a behavioural treatment programme prohibitive. They may either refuse to accept the therapy offered, or show poor co-operation and tend to drop out. Therapists usually make an effort to persuade a reluctant patient to accept the treatment offered, by answering their queries and pointing out that the chances of improvement are high. A reluctant or doubting patient is often helped by the opportunity to talk to a successfully treated patient. In the end, however, the patient must decide for himself whether or not to accept therapy. Careful cognitive therapy at the preliminary stages often facilitates treatment acceptance and co-operation. It is important to ensure that the patient is well motivated. A patient with low motivation to change is unlikely to benefit much from treatment. Such a patient is unlikely to comply fully with the instructions of a behavioural programme. In cases where a patient is pressured into therapy by family members, the results tend to be poor unless the patient himself sees the need to comply. A therapist will carefully assess a patient's motivation to accept therapy, before undertaking to treat him.

OTHER TYPES OF PSYCHOLOGICAL TREATMENT

Psychotherapy

By 'psychotherapy', we mean psychoanalysis (see pp. 51-2) or other forms of psychodynamic therapies. They share the assumption that the obsessions and/or compulsions of the patient are only symptoms of underlying unconscious problems. The aim of the therapy, done in sessions in which the patient is encouraged to talk, is to unravel these hidden factors (the 'real' problem) and resolve them. The relationship that develops between the patient and the therapist is also considered important and is said to play a part both in bringing to surface deeprooted conflicts and memories and in resolving them. A patient may be seen twice weekly, or even more frequently, for two or three years. The results of this kind of therapy have not been shown to be satisfactory, particularly for obsessive–compulsive disorder. Sometimes, a patient may report that regular psychotherapy sessions have given him a better understanding of the problems or a better outlook on life, but the specific complaints rarely improve beyond what might happen if the problem was left untreated. This form of therapy is usually available only privately, so it can be expensive.

Hypnotherapy

Claims made by some practitioners for the effectiveness of hypnotherapy, usually involving strong suggestion to the patient while under hypnosis that he will no longer have obsessions or compulsions, are not supported. There is no satisfactory evidence that hypnotherapy has much to contribute in treating these patients. Some patients and/or their families are fascinated by the very idea of hypnotherapy and ask for it when they come for help, but faith in its efficacy is misguided.

Group therapy

Treating patients in a group setting is sometimes undertaken by therapists for various conditions. For example, patients with difficulties in social skills are often treated in social skills groups. There is, as yet, no persuasive evidence that group therapy has any special role to play in the therapy of obsessive-compulsive patients. However, support groups for patients have been found to be of some benefit, when used as an adjunct to individual therapy. Family members may also be included in the support groups.

NON-PSYCHOLOGICAL TREATMENTS

Drug treatments

Many psychiatrists believe that pharmacological treatment is of considerable value in obsessive-compulsive disorder.

Sometimes, patients are given anxiolytic benzodiazepine drugs such as chlordiazepoxide (for example, Librium) or diazepam (for example, Valium). Usually, they give temporary relief from the feelings of anxiety or tension, but tend to have no effect on the obsessions or compulsions themselves. These drugs can also be habit-forming. Phenothiazenes such as chlorpromazine (for example, Largactil) are also occasionally prescribed but, again, there is seldom real benefit from them.

Antidepressant drugs are often prescribed, and varying degrees of success have been reported. In those many cases in which the obsessive-compulsive disorder is compounded by depression, direct treatment of the depression by drugs or psychological methods is needed. As noted earlier (see p. 20) a severely depressed obsessive–compulsive patient is unlikely to benefit from, or indeed effectively engage in, behavioural treatment. In such cases, the first priority is to treat the depression. In some, the successful treatment of the depression is followed by alleviation of the obsessive–compulsive problems, and additional treatment may not be necessary. In others, a reduction of the depression leaves the obsessions and compulsions weakened, but still handicapping and distressing. Additional treatment is then required.

The alleviation of depression that accompanies obsessive–compulsive disorder can be achieved by standard antidepressant medication. A list of these is given in Appendix 2.

Strong claims have been made that the tricyclic antidepressant clomipramine (Anafranil) is of particular value in the treatment of obsessive–compulsive patients. It is possible that it is particularly efficacious in reducing the depression in these patients, but whether it also has a specific effect on obsessive–compulsive disorder is still a matter for debate. In a major study carried out in London in the seventies with the support of the Medical Research Council, it was observed that clomipramine did reduce both depression and obsessive–compulsive problems in a group of patients who suffered from both. However, in those patients who had little depression, clomipramine failed to produce significant improvement. The results of more recent studies do not provide a consistent picture. On balance, the evidence points to the conclusion that clomipramine is effective, especially when depression is also present; but the improvements are seldom complete, and a significant minority of patients do not benefit from the drug. Recent research also suggests that the initial response to clomipramine does not provide a good prediction of the longer term effects of this medication. Further, patients tend to relapse when they stop taking the drug.

Common side-effects of clomipramine include: dryness of the mouth, constipation, dizziness, nausea, drowsiness, and impairment of sexual functioning—particularly, difficulty reaching orgasm.

Clomipramine is usually started with small doses, gradually increasing to 150–250 mg a day as necessary. Most patients take between

150–200 mg. The response to the medication is not immediate; it can be several weeks before any effect is seen.

Of the other antidepressant drugs tested in recent years, encouraging but not yet conclusive results have been achieved with fluoxetine (Prozac), given 20–80 mg daily, and fluvoxamine (Faverin), with an average dose of 150 mg a day and a maximum of 300 mg daily. Early reports suggest that both fluoxetine and fluvoxamine have fewer side-effects than clomipramine. The overall value of these drugs in the management of the disorder remains to be determined.

Psychosurgery

In the past, many patients with obsessive–compulsive disorder were treated with psychosurgery—that is, surgery on the brain. Psycho-surgery was originally introduced as a potential method for treating schizophrenia, and was then extended to other problems, including obsessive–compulsive disorder. The operations are used far less often now than a few decades ago.

Psychosurgery is an invasive and drastic form of treatment, although the techniques used are now much more refined than they were some decades ago, and therefore have fewer side-effects than in the early days. Also, there are several different surgical procedures that are used now-adays (unlike in the early days when the only procedure was leucotomy, which consisted of destroying a small part of the white matter of the brain in the frontal lobes). Although moderately favourable results have been claimed in some patients with chronic intractable rituals or obses-sions, in many others the results of psychosurgery have been unsatis-factory. Moreover, some patients who do report improvement say that they still have just the same obsessional thoughts and so on, but that they are less troubled by them. There is no evidence that psychosurgery is nearly as effective a form of therapy as the non-invasive psychological techniques.

Electroconvulsive therapy (ECT)

Occasionally, severe obsessive–compulsive patients have been treated with ECT (also called electric shock therapy). In this procedure, con-vulsions or fits are induced by passing a small electric current through the brain from electrodes applied to the head, while the patient is under the effects of a short-acting anaesthetic and a muscle relaxant. It is painless, and the patient retains no memory of the procedure. There is no evidence that ECT has any beneficial effects on obsessive–compulsive disorder.

TREATMENT OF OBSESSIVE-COMPULSIVE CHILDREN

The literature on the treatment of children with obsessive–compulsive disorder is thin, largely due to the relatively small number of cases reported. The best treatment seems to be the same kind of behaviour therapy used with adult patients—especially a combination of exposure and response prevention for those with overt rituals. Clomipramine is also reported to be beneficial in some cases. Parents are involved in the treatment and given advice and help on how to deal with the child's behaviour, especially his demands for things to be done in a certain way, or repeated requests for reassurance. This is an important part of therapy, as family members need a good deal of help and support. Formal family therapy may be undertaken in addition to the specific behavioural treatment; indeed, some therapists consider this to be an integral part of therapy. In some cases, the severity of the problem makes a period in hospital necessary.

8. Assessment and evaluation

In the section on the practical aspects of behavioural treatment, we discussed briefly some of the ways in which a therapist assesses obsessive–compulsive problems (see pp. 60–1). Therapists of different orientations and backgrounds will assess these problems in slightly different ways, but some aspects of assessment are nigh universal.

AIMS OF ASSESSMENT

One aim of assessment is diagnosis, and psychologists, doctors, and psychiatrists will particularly look for the diagnostic features when a patient is initially seen. The criteria commonly used in the diagnosis of this disorder are the ones we have listed in Table 1 (see p. 2). Diagnosis is usually not a problem with these patients, although there can be some puzzling cases.

Once the diagnosis is established, further and more detailed assessment is undertaken. The main purpose of this is to gather information for devising a treatment programme. As these patients are usually best treated by a behavioural approach, detailed information is needed to enable an effective treatment plan to be carried out. Behavioural therapists—whether psychologists, psychiatrists, nurse therapists, or other professionals—will therefore enquire in detail about various aspects of the problem. This is also linked to a further aim of assessment—namely, to evaluate the effects of treatment.

HOW IS ASSESSMENT DONE?

The main techniques of assessment used by therapists are summarized in the following paragraphs.

Interview with the patient

The main mode of assessment is the interview. This may take, on average, two to three hours spread over more than one session. In this, the patient will be asked for full details of the problem(s), including how they affect his work, relationships, and social life. Questions will be asked about how and when it all started and what the course of the disorder has been, including fluctuations in severity, relation to stressful events, and so on. As for the problems themselves, close enquiry will be made about each presenting problem.

For obsessions, these enquiries will focus, among others, on the following examples. What is content of the obsession? What form (that is, thought, image, or impulse, or a combination) does it take? Is it triggered by any event or object? How long does it last when it comes? How does the patient try to get rid of it? How much anxiety or discomfort does it lead to? Does it lead to a compulsion?

For compulsions, the questions will include the following examples. What events or objects lead to the urge? How strong is the urge? What is the actual nature of the compulsive behaviour? Is it an overt (motor) behaviour or a covert (mental) behaviour? How long does it last? Does it need to be performed a certain number of times? How much does the patient resist the urge? What happens if the compulsive behaviour is interrupted? What does the patient think or believe will happen if he does not carry out the compulsion? How frequently does it occur? The therapist will also ask about how much avoidance there is, whether there is any reassurance seeking and, if so, from whom, and whether any other members of the family are involved in the rituals. Normally, all the aspects of obsessive-compulsive phenomena summarized in Table 2 (see p. 13) will be gone into in some detail.

The therapist will also explore the relationship between the problems and mood, and may ask several questions about depression.

Self-ratings

Most therapists will ask the patient to rate the discomfort and the urge to ritualize on a numerical scale (see p. 60). Some use a 0-10 scale, others prefer a 0-8 scale, while still others use a 0-100 scale. The last mentioned is easy for patients to use and is recommended by many. Sometimes, especially with children, a visual analogue scale is used instead. This is simply a straight line, usually 100 mm in length, one end of which indicates the highest possible level of what is being measured (such as extremely high discomfort), and the other the absence of it (for example, no discomfort at all). The patient indicates where, on this line, his response lies. The therapist can convert this into a numerical score by simply measuring the distance from the 'low' end to the place marked by the patient, as in Fig. 1.

Fig. 1. A visual analogue scale sometimes used for rating discomfort.

No discomfort _____ Extremely high
    at all   discomfort

In preparation for therapy, various situations (for example, using a public telephone or leaving the house without checking gas taps) that are relevant to the patient's problems will be listed, with ratings of discomfort and of compulsive urge. For each main problem, a separate list or hierarchy may be prepared. An example of such a list was given in Table 3 (see p. 61).

Interviewing others

Interviewing a family member or other key informant is also part of the assessment, whenever possible. Some aspects of the patient's problems are often more clearly described by a family member than by the patient himself. For example, the problems and stresses caused by the patient's behaviour and demands on the family may be minimized in the patient's own account. Sometimes a patient has no realistic idea of the extent of his own disability, and information from the family or other informants will be most valuable. Occasionally, information may be sought from work colleagues or employers. Contact with family and employers is made only with the patient's consent.

In the case of children, needless to say, interviewing parents is not just beneficial but essential. One may have to rely heavily on parents for basic information about the presenting problem, especially in the early stages of assessment.

Behavioural tests and direct observation

Sometimes a therapist may carry out one or more behavioural tests with the patient. For example, a patient with contamination fears about dirt and germs on door handles, public telephones, and so on, may be asked to touch a door handle during the interview season. The patient's reaction, his attempts to avoid this, and his rating of the discomfort felt while carrying out the action, are all important information for the therapist. Behavioural tests may be carried out at home or, less frequently, at work. Direct observation at home or at work may also be undertaken. For example, a man whose obsessional slowness began to severely affect his efficiency at work was observed by the therapist for a set period of time, with prior arrangement.

Record keeping by the patient

It is common for a therapist to ask the patient to keep a daily record of his problem behaviour for a week or two prior to starting therapy, as a baseline measure. It may be continued during therapy as a way of monitoring progress. The record can either be an open-ended account in which the patient writes in detail what happens, or—more commonly—a record using a structured format provided by the therapist. An example of a structured record form is given in Fig. 2 and a completed record form in Fig. 3. As can be seen, the record focuses on selected target problems which are briefly recorded. Such structured records are easier to use and much more amenable to analysis than open-ended accounts. Another problem with open-ended accounts is that many obsessive–compulsive patients religiously write pages and pages of detail. One patient who was asked to keep a written record of his daily problems for a week produced a sheaf of over a hundred pages in very small, neat handwriting!

Questionnaires and inventories

Standard questionnaires and similar instruments are also used in assessment. These have the advantage of covering a range of difficulties and producing a numerical summary score. These are, however, not used as a substitute for interview, but during interview as an additional measure. Checklists, questionnaires, and inventories are often used in this way. Some patients find it extremely difficult to respond to questionnaire items, and spend hours agonizing over the precise accuracy of their replies. If the completion of the questionnaires takes excessive time or is upsetting, they can be omitted or delayed.

Fig. 2. An example of a daily record sheet, blank.

Date: Target:[1]

Time	Frequency[2]	Highest discomfort[3]	Highest compulsive urge[4]	Details and comments[5]
Before 7 a.m.				
7–10 a.m.				
10 a.m.– 1 p.m.				
1–4 p.m.				
4–7 p.m.				
7–10 p.m.				
After 10 p.m.				

1   The particular obsession or compulsion monitored.

2   How many times it happened in each time period.

3,4 Rated on a 0–100 scale; give the highest felt during the time period.

5   Details of what happened: when, where, what was the trigger, how long taken, number of repetitions, and so on, of the worst episode.

Three commonly used instruments are described below.

The Maudsley Obsessional–Compulsive Inventory

A widely used self-report instrument for obsessive–compulsive patients is the *Maudsley Obsessional–Compulsive Inventory* (MOCI), which was developed in the seventies at the Maudsley Hospital, in London. The

Fig. 3. An example of a daily record sheet, completed.

Date: 27 September   Target:[1] Handwashing

Time	Frequency[2]	Highest discomfort[3]	Highest compulsive urge[4]	Details and comments[5]
Before 7 a.m.	2	70	70	After using toilet. Washed hands with soap, 3 mins.
7–10 a.m.	3	80	85	After journey to work by bus. Felt quite dirty. Washed with soap, 4 mins.
10 a.m.– 1 p.m.	0			In office all the time.
1–4 p.m.	2	60	60	After going to the toilet. Washed with soap, 3 mins.
4–7 p.m.	3	85	90	Felt very dirty after return journey in crowded bus. Washed with soap, 5 mins.
7–10 p.m.	1	40	45	Before supper. Washed without soap, 1 min.
After 10 p.m.	2	70	75	After cleaning toilet. Washed with soap, also arms, 5 mins.

1   The particular obsession or compulsion monitored.

2   How many times it happened in each time period.

3,4 Rated on a 0–100 scale; give the highest felt during the time period.

5   Details of what happened: when, where, what was the trigger, how long taken, number of repetitions, and so on, of the <u>worst</u> episode.

MOCI consists of 30 items. The patient has to choose either 'true' or 'false' for each item. The inventory yields an overall obsessive-compulsive symptom score, and in addition separate subscores for checking, washing and cleaning, slowness and repetitiveness, and doubting and conscientiousness.

These are a few items from the MOCI:

- I avoid using public telephones because of possible contamination.
- I use only an average amount of soap.
- Some numbers are extremely unlucky.
- One of my major problems is that I pay too much attention to detail.

The full inventory and the scoring key are reproduced in Appendix 3 and Appendix 4.

The MOCI is easy to use, and has been shown to be a useful part of the assessment. It has been established as a standard instrument in several countries.

The Leyton Obsessional Inventory

The MOCI deals with obsessive–compulsive symptoms only. The *Leyton Obsessional Inventory* (LOI), on the other hand, covers symptoms and obsessional personality traits. The LOI, developed by John Cooper in London, has 69 items, 46 of which deal with symptoms and the rest with personality features. It yields four scores: symptoms, traits, interference, and resistance. The LOI is usually administered with the items typed on cards, each of which the patient puts into either the box for 'yes' or the box for 'no', although some therapists now use paper and pencil versions of the test. The administration and the scoring are more time consuming than for the MOCI. There is also a children's version of the LOI consisting of 44 items.

A few sample items from the LOI are:

- Do you ever have persistent imaginings that your children or husband/wife might be having an accident or that something might have happened to them?
- Do you ever have to go back and check doors, cupboards or windows to make sure that they are really shut?
- Do you dislike brushing against people or being touched in any way?
- Do you take great care in hanging and folding your clothes at night?

The Compulsive Activity Checklist

This instrument is used both for self-rating by the patient, and for rating by the therapist. The *Compulsive Activity Checklist* (CAC) lists 39 specific activities (for example, having a bath or shower, brushing teeth, cleaning the house, switching lights and taps on or off, touching door handles, filling in forms, eating in restaurants, and throwing things away). Each activity is rated on a 4-point scale of severity, from 0 (no problem with the activity) to 3 (unable to complete or attempt the activity). A total score is obtained by adding the scores of the individual items. The total score, however, is less important than the range of activities that present problems in the patient's life, and the identification of those activities that are impossible or extremely difficult to complete.

The CAC was developed in the seventies at the Maudsley Hospital, in London. It is used regularly in many clinics and hospitals.

Other instruments

The therapist may also use other inventories to measure depression, anxiety, phobias, and so on, if there is an indication that these are relevant in a patient's clinical presentation. As noted previously (see p. 20), depression tends to be closely linked to obsessions and compulsions, and many therapists include it in routine assessment. The most widely used screening instrument for assessing depression is the *Beck Depression Inventory*. Developed by Aaron T. Beck and his colleagues, it comprises 21 items covering areas such as mood, self-esteem, sleep, appetite, feelings of guilt, suicidal ideas, and so on. For each item, the patient is asked to indicate whether he has experienced the effect or change and, if so, to what degree. Scores of 0–3 are obtained for each item, yielding a possible maximum of 63. A score of 18 is usually taken as a rough cut-off point, indicating significant depression.

Psychophysiological assessment

Psychophysiological measures are sometimes undertaken with obsessive-compulsive patients. Activity of the autonomic nervous system, especially heart rate and skin conductance, may be measured under various conditions—for example, while exposed to triggers, and after carrying out a compulsive ritual. While such measures are valuable for research, their usefulness in routine clinical assessment is limited. In most clinical settings, patients will not be asked to undergo these recordings.

ASSESSMENT FOR EVALUATING THERAPY

In a systematic therapeutic approach, the patient will be assessed in some or all of the above ways at several points in time: before treatment begins, after a period of therapy, at the end of therapy, and at follow-up usually six and twelve months later. In this way, the patient's progress can be ascertained formally and methodically. The numerical scores, in particular, help to highlight the changes in the patient. For example, assuming successful therapy, a patient whose MOCI score was 21 at initial assessment may have a score of 7 at the six-month follow-up. A situation that evoked a discomfort level of 90 (on a 0–100 scale) before therapy may not provoke more than 10 any more. The frequency of handwashing, which was twelve times a day on average before therapy, may now be only two per day.

9. Some practical advice

IS THERE A PROBLEM?

Although the majority of people have obsessional experiences and compulsions, for most people these are not major problems. The person is not particularly worried or concerned about them, and neither seeks nor wants assistance. There is no evidence that Samuel Johnson (see p. 10) was particularly bothered about his ritual concerning the number of steps to take when approaching a door. If you check your gas cooker twice before you leave home every morning, or tend to be a bit concerned about cleanliness and make sure that you wash your hands before each meal, there is no need to feel that there is something faulty or abnormal in your behaviour. Similarly, if you get the occasional unwanted thought, 'God does not exist', or an occasional mental image of a corpse in a coffin, again that need not worry you. It is not the mere presence of obsessions and/or compulsions that warrants concern; rather, it is whether they interfere with your life and activities in a significant way, and whether they cause you distress.

Some key questions

So, the questions that you need to ask yourself are such as the following:

- Are there things that you very much like or need to do, but are prevented from doing, because of your obsessions and/or compulsions?
- Do you find yourself constantly avoiding certain things, places, people, and activities as a result of obsessions and/or compulsions?
- Has your job or other occupation become difficult as a result of obsessions and/or compulsions?
- Do you get very upset by the content or frequency of the obsessions?
- Are you very unhappy about the nature of your compulsive rituals—for example, are they bizarre or very excessive, or do they make you open to ridicule by others?

- Do you find yourself spending a great deal of your time engaging in compulsive behaviour or obsessional ruminations?
- Is your compulsive behaviour a significant nuisance or hindrance to others?

If your answers to any of these questions is 'yes', then it is possible that your obsessions and/or compulsions merit attention, and you may wish to consider doing something about them.

Concern about a family member

The same considerations apply when a spouse, parent, or any other relative or friend notices compulsive behaviour, excessive reassurance seeking, and so on in a person. It may be that someone takes a little more time in the bath than other members of the family, or has his room arranged in a particularly neat way. This should not worry the family. On the other hand, if the behaviour is very excessive, the person consistently makes unreasonable demands on the family, or it is clear that his work is seriously affected, then the family may be justifiably worried and want to initiate some action. Many people with obsessive-compulsive problems attempt to hide their difficulties from their families and friends, so it may not become clear to them in the early stages that a problem exists.

SEEKING HELP

Once it is recognized that there is a problem, the best course of action is to seek professional advice. In some cases, it may be possible to deal with the difficulties without recourse to such help (see below, pp. 96–102), but in most cases seeking professional advice is the best action.

Finding a therapist

The first step is to go to your own doctor and explain the problem. There is no need to fear that he will think you are peculiar or crazy; he will recognize that this is a problem requiring help, and refer you to a professional who is skilled in dealing with it. This will usually be a clinical psychologist or a psychiatrist or, where available, a nurse therapist with special training in dealing with problems of this kind. Exceptionally, your doctor may himself give you advice and treatment, if he has a particular interest and experience in this area.

The psychologist or psychiatrist to whom you are referred is likely to be someone with a behavioural approach, in view of the success of this approach in dealing with these problems. If the doctor is unaware of a suitable therapist locally, you or your doctor could contact the British Association for Behavioural Psychotherapy (BABP), who will advise on therapists in the area. This will, however, be unnecessary in most cases, because the local psychiatric hospital will normally be able to channel you to a suitable practitioner. Most of these therapists are in the National Health Service in Britain but if, for some reason, you prefer to see someone privately, the BABP will be able to advise. General advice on the services of clinical psychologists and psychiatrists may be obtained from their respective professional organizations, the British Psychological Society and the Royal College of Psychiatrists. Advice is also obtainable from MIND, which is the National Association for Mental Health, and the organization called Phobic Action.

In the United States, the OCD Foundation, set up a few years ago, provides information and advice for sufferers of obsessive–compulsive disorder and their families and friends. Many have found contact with the foundation, which is a voluntary and non-profit-making organization, to be extremely useful. Another organization that provides useful information and advice on this disorder is the Anxiety Disorders Association of America.

The addresses of these agencies are given in Appendix 5.

The therapist's assessment

When you go for your initial assessment, the therapist will try to collect as much relevant information as possible. It may well take more than one interview for him to complete the assessment. The information he is likely to request will include the kind of detail we have discussed in the previous chapters, especially the one on assessment (see pp. 80–8). Your therapist may also give you some questionnaires, checklists, or inventories to complete. He may ask you to carry out short tests. For example, if your problems include a fear of contamination by dirt he may ask you to touch, with an open palm of your hand, table surfaces, tops of cupboards, and so on. Or, if you have horrific thoughts and impulses that you might stab someone, the therapist may ask you to hold a knife or pair of scissors in your hands and to describe to him what thoughts, images, and impulses come to your mind at the time. He may also give you some homework in the form of keeping a diary or record of your problems as they occur in the next week or two. Co-operate with this even if you think it is a chore. The therapist is also likely to want to interview a family member or friend, and you may be asked to arrange this. He may also want to see you at home, to see for himself what your problems are and how you cope. Naturally, this will depend on the nature of the problem and on how much time the therapist has at his disposal. Many therapists nowadays, if they can find the time, are likely to include a home visit as part of the assessment, especially when you have rituals which you carry out at home or home-related avoidance behaviour.

Planning and implementation of therapy

In planning the treatment programme, your therapist will discuss with you what areas to concentrate on, what targets to be aimed for, and how to set about achieving these targets. The involvement of a family member as a cotherapist is likely to be discussed, and he or she will be included in the discussion of homework arrangements and related matters. If the problem is difficult to manage on an out-patient basis, hospitalization for a limited period will be considered. Hospital treatment will include not only your therapist, but nurses and other professionals as well. A family member may also be invited to take part in some hospital sessions, who can then help with the next stage of therapy away from hospital. If your treatment is entirely on an out-patient basis, as is quite possible, the therapist may conduct, or arrange for, some additional sessions in your home. These domiciliary sessions can be extremely valuable, and many therapists consider them to be essential. Irrespective of this, you will be given plenty of advice and instructions about what you should and should not do at home. For example, you may be told that you should not wash at all, except for a daily five-minute shower; or that you should disarrange your desk and wardrobe and leave them like that. The implementation of such instructions will be left to you and/or the family member acting as cotherapist.

Do not be surprised if the therapist asks you to continue to keep regular records of what happens at home, as this information is valuable in monitoring your progress. He may wish to go over your home records and discuss them in detail at the beginning of each session.

If an exposure and response prevention programme is undertaken in an out-patient clinic, at least some of your sessions with the therapist are likely to be quite long. This is because the therapist will want to ensure a significantly long response prevention period to allow your discomfort to dissipate. Also, part of each session is likely to be devoted to discussions between you and the therapist. He may wish to explore your fears of disaster, your difficulties in home work, what you really think will happen if you do not ritualize, and so on. There may also be imaginal exposure. For example, if your fears include a worry that, if you do not check the gas taps three times, the whole house will burn down, your therapist may ask you to close your eyes and very vividly imagine such a scene. Such imaginal exposure may be conducted in several sessions. At times, real-life exposure to a particular situation may be preceded by you being asked to go through the experience in your imagination.

In sum, your sessions are likely to be lengthy (especially at the start), and also to include various activities. The main ingredient, however, will be exposure and response prevention, if your main problems are treatable in this way, along with detailed homework instructions. If your main problems are of a different kind, such as repetitive unwanted thoughts with no associated overt rituals, then your treatment sessions will take a different form. Even then, homework is very likely to be part of the programme. If your main problem is slowness, then much of the therapy may well be home-based.

A further word is needed about the involvement of family members. The role that a cotherapist plays will be clearly defined and detailed, and specific instructions given. This is in order to avoid any ambiguity leading to conflict. The family will also receive instructions about not complying with your demands, or requests for reassurance. All of these will have been discussed fully and openly with your active involvement. Any doubts or queries you may have, you should discuss fully with the therapist.

The need for co-operation

It is important that you co-operate fully with the therapist, your co-therapist, and any others involved. Carrying out some of the instructions may be very difficult for you (for example, the task of rubbing your hands on the kitchen floor and then not washing your hands) but it is important that you do your best to comply. The difficulty will, normally, get progressively less with more and more sessions. If you find that you are sometimes tempted not to comply fully—for example, you may feel like washing your hands secretly, or touching the floor only very lightly with the tips of your fingers—it is important that you discuss it with the therapist. Remember that therapy for these problems is essentially a joint venture. Your therapist has no magic cure, and without your co-operation can achieve nothing. Half-hearted co-operation will only waste your time as well as your therapist's. So discuss any problems with him. He will appreciate your difficulties, and discuss them with you. If, for some reason, you wash when you are not supposed to, you can remedy this to some extent by immediately 'recontaminating' yourself by touching the contaminating object.

It can, in short, be difficult work. But, if you are motivated to get over your problems, you will find that, with the help of your therapist, you can keep it up. Occasional lapses should not be seen as failure. Do not let them discourage you. Once you begin to see the results of your efforts, you will be very glad that you underwent the therapy. It will make a big difference.

Adjustment problems

When you gradually improve with treatment, you may well find that you need to adjust to a new lifestyle, especially if your problems have been longstanding. You will find much free time, and probably not many activities to fill that time with. You will need to develop new ways of filling your time, and perhaps new activities. You may need to re-establish old contacts and relationships. Your therapist will usually discuss these matters with you and also give advice and counselling on how to make these adjustments. It is possible that your family members will also have similar problems, if their lives had been moulded around your problems.

After therapy

When you have achieved improvement, do not expect to be totally free of symptoms. What usually happens, in cases where the problem involves interrelated obsessions and compulsions, is that the compulsive behaviour is brought under control with the exposure and response prevention treatment fairly rapidly, but the obsessional ideas may not go away at the same time. They may linger on, but without arousing much discomfort or leading to a strong compulsive urge. After a time, you will notice them less and less, and they may well disappear altogether. You may still have minor residual problems, and perhaps continue to be a more anxious person than many others. Do not be too disappointed at this—you can learn to cope with these. With the major disabling problems largely out of the way, such coping will be easier.

Once successfully treated, the chances of a major relapse are not very high. However, there may be minor lapses. At times of stress (for example, with problems at work and so on) the chances of symptoms reappearing may be somewhat increased. You can minimize the effects of stress if you use strategies to cope with situations. Relaxation practice is one such strategy (see Appendix 1). If symptoms of the disorder do reappear, you will notice these signs early on, and can give yourself a few booster sessions using the principles of treatment you are now familiar with. It is also not unusual for a therapist to have arranged boosters at various time intervals. He will, in any case, have arranged for follow-up appointments for you, in order to ascertain how well you are doing and to give you help and support as needed. If you feel that you are losing control again, contact your therapist, even if there is no follow-up arrangement. It must be reiterated, however, that, after a carefully planned behaviour therapy programme has been successfully carried out, the chances of the problems re-emerging in full-blown form are limited.

The use of drugs

It is possible that your therapist will consider drugs as part of the treatment. As only a medical practitioner can prescribe drugs, if your therapist is not a doctor he will ask your own doctor, or a psychiatrist he works with, to consider this. The most likely circumstances for this would be if your mood is depressed and this has either stalled your progress or is making it difficult for you even to engage in the therapy. In such cases, antidepressant medication may be prescribed (see pp. 77–8). Or, your doctor may want to start the treatment of your obsessions and compulsions with a drug. Whatever drug is prescribed, it is very important that you tell the doctor what other medicines you are taking, any allergies that you have, whether you are pregnant, and so on. Make sure you get very clear instructions about the dosage and what foods and drinks (if any) to avoid, and discuss possible side-effects. Commonly prescribed antidepressant drugs, including clomipramine, have several well-known side-effects (see p. 77). These are, however, reversible: when the drug is stopped, they will clear up.

Two other points are worth bearing in mind with regard to medication. The first is that antidepressant drugs do not produce results immediately—it may be weeks before any improvement is seen. Second, if you are treated just with an antidepressant drug and no behavioural treatment, improvements in your obsessive–compulsive symptoms may diminish or disappear when you come off the drug.

If you are on anxiety-reducing drugs at the time of seeking help from a behaviour therapist, he may suggest that you discuss with the prescriber whether the drugs should be withdrawn or at least reduced, before therapy begins. The prescribing doctor will be fully involved in these discussions and decisions. If you are in the habit of drinking high amounts of alcohol, you will be asked to reduce this.

Brain surgery

It is extremely unlikely that your therapist will recommend brain surgery—unless your problems are very chronic, totally resistant to other forms of therapy, and you are incapacitated by them, this will not even be considered. If psychosurgery *is* proposed, you do not have to agree to accept this procedure and you would be well advised to seek a second or even a third opinion, if you wish to consider it. Even then, the final decision will be yours alone. Normally, this form of treatment is best avoided. When it is suggested, the very fullest consultation and discussion are needed.

SELF-TREATMENT

Is it possible for someone with obsessive–compulsive disorder to treat himself? Recent research done in a major London hospital has shown that some patients treating themselves do almost as well as those treated by therapists; but, in this case, the assessment and initial advice came from qualified and experienced therapists. Can you do the whole thing yourself, from start to finish? If the problem is not very severe, and if there are no other complications, this is not impossible. You need a commitment to the planned treatment, and a systematic approach. If you are seriously depressed, however, then you should not attempt this. Also, if you habitually take a lot of alcohol or drugs such as benzodiazepines, self-help should not be attempted without first consulting your doctor. The nature of the problem is also important. Clear overt rituals, and clear avoidance behaviour which is well defined, are likely to be more amenable to self-treatment than incessant ruminations or complicated mental rituals. You need to decide whether yours is the right kind of problem to treat yourself.

Selecting targets

The first requirement is to select and specify a small number of targets related to your problem. Consider what aspects of the problem you need to improve in most, then formulate the target very specifically. For example, you may decide that one of your targets will be 'to be able to empty the kitchen waste bin into the main dustbin each night' or 'to be able to leave home every morning without checking the gas and electricity more than once'. These are good, workable targets. More global targets such as 'to get rid of my fear of contamination' or 'to be free of repeated checking and doubting' are less useful, and hard to make use of in treatment programmes. So, be specific in setting targets for yourself.

Do not attempt to tackle too many targets at once. It is advisable to begin with just one, or two at the most. As therapy progresses, you can add on new targets to your programme as you master the original targets.

Getting the help of others

If at all possible, enlist the help of a cotherapist, to whom you will explain your problems and the therapy plan fully. The cotherapist may be your wife or husband, a relative living at home or nearby, or a friend or a trusted colleague, for certain kinds of targets. It is a good idea to write down with your cotherapist exactly what his role will be, and your commitments to him (for example, not to argue when he reminds you to do something). Obviously, if your problems involve others being asked to comply with your demands or to provide you with reassurance and so on, then they need to be told not to comply any more, in relation to the targets you are working on.

Record-keeping

Keeping records is important. They make it easier for you to see your progress, and to identify any difficulties that may arise. For a start, it will be useful to just monitor yourself for a two-week period, using a form like the one in Figs 2 and 3 (see pp. 84 and 85). This will give you a record of the extent of the problem prior to treatment. For recording your actual treatment, use another record sheet—like the specimen form given in Fig. 4. Figure 5 is an illustration of a completed sheet. You will see how all the main details can be recorded on such a form systematically and without too much effort.

Fig. 4. A specimen record sheet for a treatment session, blank.

Date: Target:[1]

Task[2]	
Time	
Any help[3]	
Discomfort felt[4]	
Urge to ritualize[5]	
Outcome[6]	

1 The particular compulsion treated.

2 Specific task undertaken.

3 Was a cotherapist involved? Who?

4,5 Rated on a 0–100 scale.

6 Details of what happened.

Fig. 5. An example of a completed record sheet for a treatment session.

Date: 10 October   **Target:**[1] Handwashing

Task[2]	Take kitchen waste bin downstairs and empty into main bin. Clean and reline kitchen bin and place it back in kitchen. Rub hands on clothes and arms. No washing or wiping.
Time	9.15 a. m.
Any help[3]	Frances (girlfriend) accompanied me downstairs and back, and encouraged me to rub my hands on my clothes and arms.
Discomfort felt[4]	80 (half-hourly ratings on separate form)
Urge to ritualize[5]	75 (as above)
Outcome[6]	Kept my hands loosely clenched and sat in a corner for some time. Gradually felt better. Had some tea about 10.30. Read the newspaper. On the whole, it went well.

1   The particular compulsion treated.

2   Specific task undertaken.

3   Was a cotherapist involved? Who?

4,5 Rated on a 0–100 scale.

6   Details of what happened.

In addition, for each exposure session, you can monitor and record your discomfort and urge to ritualize in graphic form. An easy-to-use format for this is provided in Fig 6. An example of a completed form is given in Fig. 7.

Fig. 6. A specimen sheet for recording discomfort and urge to ritualize in an exposure and response prevention session.

Discomfort and urge to ritualize (0–100)

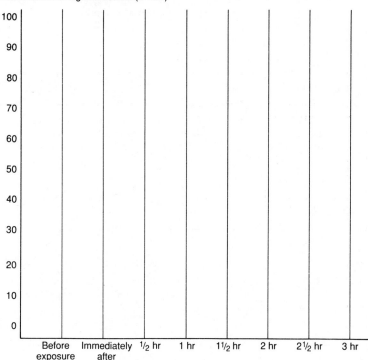

Record level of discomfort with an X, and strength of urge to ritualize with an O; connect each set of entries.

Implementing therapy

For your exposure sessions, you will need to allow some time, even up to three hours for major tasks. It is best not to finish a session while your discomfort is still high, so make sure that you have enough time. For many other tasks, much less time will be needed. It is best to start with difficult but manageable tasks. If you start with tasks that are too difficult, you may end up getting discouraged. For some targets, especially where

Fig. 7. An example of a completed sheet for recording discomfort and urge to ritualize in an exposure and response prevention session.

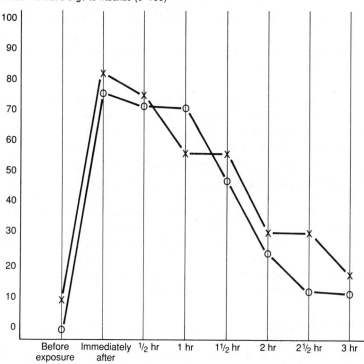

Discomfort and urge to ritualize (0–100)

Before exposure | Immediately after | ½ hr | 1 hr | 1½ hr | 2 hr | 2½ hr | 3 hr

Record level of discomfort with an X, and strength of urge to ritualize with an O; connect each set of entries.

the problem consists of time-consuming rituals, a gradual step-by-step approach may be appropriate. If, for example, one of your problems is spending over an hour in folding and hanging your clothes at night, your target may be 'folding and hanging my clothes at night in ten minutes'. If you are happy to attempt this from the very first day, then fine. On the other hand, if it is too much to attempt at first, you could break this target down into a series of tasks; you will set yourself the task of completing the activity in progressively shorter time each night. For example, on day one, forty minutes; day two, thirty minutes; day three, twenty minutes, and so on. Remember, however, that a long series of very small steps is not a very efficient way of going about your targets, so do try to start at a fairly high level.

Always remember the basic principles of exposure and response prevention—the less you avoid things because of your obsession or through fear of having to ritualize, the better. So, in addition to your formal programme, make sure that you confront your difficulties or obstacles rather than avoid or escape from them.

If you tend to be generally anxious, and experience marked physical signs of anxiety, then a useful addition to your self-treatment programme would be some training in relaxation. If you do this, make sure you find the time to practice regularly. How to go about teaching yourself to relax is discussed in Appendix 1.

Appraisal of problem

How you see your problem is important. Having obsessions and compulsions is not particularly unusual or rare, so remind yourself that lots of people have them (see pp. 9–10) and that having them does not mean that you are crazy or mad, or that you are going mad. The main problem is the interference they cause in your life, and this is what your treatment programme is intended to reduce.

A word of caution

A word of caution is needed about self-treatment: even if much of the therapy is done by yourself, it is useful to have your problems assessed by, and advice from, a qualified therapist. He will advise you on whether or not a self-therapy programme is suitable, and may agree to see you from time to time to review your progress. So, do not undertake it entirely on your own unless your problems are relatively minor ones, or you have no suitable therapist available. As noted earlier, once you have been seen by a therapist and a treatment plan is drawn up, a good deal of the actual work will be done by you anyway. In that sense, much of therapy for these problems nowadays necessarily involves self-treatment. The principles outlined in this section will, we hope, be of some use to you, even if you are treated by a professional therapist.

Appendix 1

LEARNING TO RELAX: A SIMPLE GUIDE

Do your relaxation exercises in a quiet room, at a time when you are not likely to be disturbed. Sit comfortably in an armchair. Make sure that your clothes are not tight. Remove belts, spectacles, and so on. Remove your shoes.

Learn to relax by first tensing and then relaxing various muscle groups of the body, one at a time. Keep your eyes closed throughout. At each step, keep the muscles tensed, quite hard, for 6-8 seconds. Concentrate on the muscles, and notice the tension. Then relax the muscles, and keep them relaxed for 45-50 seconds. Again, concentrate on the muscles, and notice how the feelings of relaxation differ from those of tension. You can learn to time yourself quite easily by slowly counting for the first few times. Remember to repeat the tense-relax cycle for each muscle group before you move on to the next. When you tense a group of muscles, take in a breath and hold it until you relax the muscles, releasing the breath slowly as you relax.

Given below is the order in which to tense and relax the various muscle groups. For each muscle group, a strategy for making them tense is given. For some, alternative strategies are suggested. Before you actually start the proper relaxation exercises, learn the way in which each muscle group can be effectively tensed. Try out one at a time, and master it. Where alternatives are suggested, decide which one is going to be your regular strategy. Once this is done, you can begin the actual sessions.

1. *Right hand and forearm* Tense the muscles by making a tight fist; or, try pressing the inner part of the finger tips against the base of the thumb. Relax by slowly opening the hand.

2. *Right biceps*   Tense the muscles by pushing your elbow into the arm of the chair, or by pressing the elbow and the upper arm into the side of the rib cage. Relax by returning to original position.

3. *Left hand and forearm*   As for right hand and forearm.

4. *Left biceps*   As for right biceps.

Note   If you are left handed, do steps 3 and 4 first, followed by steps 1 and 2.

5. *Forehead*   Tense by raising your eyebrows as high as possible with your eyes still closed. Relax by returning eyebrows to normal position.

6. *Upper cheeks and nose*   Tense by squinting and screwing up your eyes, and wrinkling the nose. Relax by returning to normal state.

7. *Lower cheeks and jaws*   Tense by clenching your teeth together and pulling back the corners of your mouth. Relax by unclenching the teeth and bringing mouth back to normal.

8. *Neck*   Tense by pulling your chin into your chest, but not quite touching it. Relax by returning to original position.

9. *Shoulder and chest*   Tense by raising and pulling your shoulder blades towards each other. Relax by returning to original position.

10. *Stomach and abdomen*   Tense by pulling in your stomach and abdomen as much as you can. You can also tense these muscles by pushing out your stomach and abdomen. Relax by returning to original state.

11. *Right leg*   Tense by straightening the whole leg from the hip, parallel to the floor. Relax by lowering and resting the leg on the floor again.

12. *Right foot*   Tense by pushing your heel into the floor and curling your toes upwards—that is, towards you. Relax by returning to original position.

13. *Left leg*   As for right leg.

14. *Left foot*   As for right foot.

Note   If your dominant leg is the left one, do steps 13 and 14 before 11 and 12.

15. *Whole body*   Tense as many of the above muscle groups as you can all at once, making yourself into a 'ball of tension'. You will find that you can tense most of the muscle groups together; in fact,

if you use the tension strategies suggested above, there will be only two of these items that you will not be able to do while doing everything else. One is the raising of the eyebrows, but the eyebrows can be tensed by wrinkling them when you screw up the eyes. The second is the pushing of your heels into the floor, but with your legs stretched, you will still be able to curl your toes up towards you.

Remember that each step is to be done twice, including the last 'all-body' step. Remember also to take in a breath and hold it when the muscles are kept tense and to release the breath as you relax the muscles.

After the whole sequence is completed, continue to sit in a relaxed state for several minutes. At this point, you may imagine a pleasant scene, like a nice beach or a flower garden. With practice, when you become more skilled in relaxing yourself, you will find that the actual exercises become quite easy. After some weeks of practice, you will be able to relax yourself by simply tensing and relaxing the entire body—that is, the last step of the sequence given above—without going through the various individual steps. With even more practice, many people acquire the ability to relax very effectively simply by concentrating on making their muscles relaxed without having first to tense them.

If you prefer to do your relaxation exercises lying down on a bed or the floor, you need only minor changes to the above programme. For each leg, what you will need to do is to raise it from the bed or floor to form an angle of about 30 degrees. Relax by lowering and resting the leg on the bed or floor.

There is no particular time of the day when relaxation should be practised but avoid doing it when you are very sleepy, to avoid falling asleep while relaxing. Try to do it daily in the early stages, so you will quickly become good at it.

There are different sequences of muscle groups suggested by different authors for relaxation exercises. There is no particular advantage of one over the others. What is important is to use a sequence which is fairly logical, as the one given here, not a random or haphazard one. You should use the same sequence regularly, so it will be easier to learn and master it.

There are cassette tapes available commercially, which give recorded instructions for relaxation training. Using one of these can be useful in the early stages, but it is important to gradually wean yourself away from the cassette, as the aim is to learn to relax without any external aid.

The following are some good cassettes that are commercially available.

Robert Sharpe's cassette *Relax and enjoy it*, which is available from Aleph One Ltd, The Old Courthouse, High Street, Bottisham, Cambridge CB5 9BA.

Jane Madders's cassette *Self-help relaxation*, available from Relaxation for Living Ltd, 29 Burwood Park Road, Walton-on-Thames, Surrey KT12 5LH.

Roy Bailey's cassette *Systematic relaxation pack*, which comes with a booklet, produced by Winslow Press Ltd, 9 London Lane, London E8 3PR.

Appendix 2

ANTIDEPRESSANT DRUGS

Drug	UK brand name	US brand name
Tricyclics		
Clomipramine	Anafranil	Anafranil
Amitriptyline	Tryptizol	Elavil
	Elavil	Amitid
		Endep
Imipramine	Tofranil	Tofranil
		SK-pramine
		Janimine
Monoamine Oxidase Inhibitors		
Phenelzine	Nardil	Nardil
Tranylcypromine	Parnate	Parnate
Isocarboxazid	Marplan	Marplan
Others		
Fluoxetine	Prozac	Prozac
Fluvoxamine	Faverin	

Note This is not a complete list.

Appendix 3

THE MAUDSLEY OBSESSIONAL-COMPULSIVE INVENTORY (MOCI)

(See Appendix 4 for scoring instructions.)

Instructions

Please answer each question by putting a circle around the TRUE or the FALSE following the question. There are no right or wrong answers, and no trick questions. Work quickly and do not think too long about the exact meaning of the question.

1. I avoid using public telephones because of possible contamination. TRUE FALSE

2. I frequently get nasty thoughts and have difficulty in getting rid of them. TRUE FALSE

3. I am more concerned than most people about honesty. TRUE FALSE

4. I am often late because I can't seem to get through everything on time. TRUE FALSE

5. I don't worry unduly about contamination if I touch an animal. TRUE FALSE

6. I frequently have to check things (for example, gas or water taps, doors, and so on) several times. TRUE FALSE

7. I have a very strict conscience. TRUE FALSE

8. I find that almost every day I am upset by unpleasant thoughts that come into my mind against my will.   TRUE   FALSE

9. I do not worry unduly if I accidentally bump into somebody.   TRUE   FALSE

10. I usually have serious doubts about the simple everyday things I do.   TRUE   FALSE

11. Neither of my parents was very strict during my childhood.   TRUE   FALSE

12. I tend to get behind in my work because I repeat things over and over again.   TRUE   FALSE

13. I use only an average amount of soap.   TRUE   FALSE

14. Some numbers are extremely unlucky.   TRUE   FALSE

15. I do not check letters over and over again before mailing them.   TRUE   FALSE

16. I do not take a long time to dress in the morning.   TRUE   FALSE

17. I am not excessively concerned about cleanliness.   TRUE   FALSE

18. One of my major problems is that I pay too much attention to detail.   TRUE   FALSE

19. I can use well-kept toilets without any hesitation.   TRUE   FALSE

20. My major problem is repeated checking.   TRUE   FALSE

21. I am not unduly concerned about germs and diseases.   TRUE   FALSE

22. I do not tend to check things more than once.   TRUE   FALSE

23. I do not stick to a very strict routine when doing ordinary things.   TRUE   FALSE

24. My hands do not feel dirty after touching money.   TRUE   FALSE

25. I do not usually count when doing a routine task.　　TRUE　　FALSE

26. I take rather a long time to complete my washing in the morning.　　TRUE　　FALSE

27. I do not use a great deal of antiseptics.　　TRUE　　FALSE

28. I spend a lot of time every day checking things over and over again.　　TRUE　　FALSE

29. Hanging and folding my clothes at night does not take up a lot of time.　　TRUE　　FALSE

30. Even when I do something very carefully, I often feel that it is not quite right.　　TRUE　　FALSE

Appendix 4

SCORING KEY FOR THE MAUDSLEY OBSESSIONAL-COMPULSIVE INVENTORY

Instructions

Score 1 when a response matches that of this key and 0 when it does not; maximum scores for the five scales are, therefore, respectively 30, 9, 11, 7, 7.

Question	Total obsessional score	Checking	Washing	Slowness-repetition	Doubting-conscientiousness
Q1	TRUE	—	TRUE	—	—
Q2	TRUE	TRUE	—	FALSE	—
Q3	TRUE	—	—	—	TRUE
Q4	TRUE	—	TRUE	TRUE	—
Q5	FALSE	—	FALSE	—	—
Q6	TRUE	TRUE	—	—	—
Q7	TRUE	—	—	—	TRUE
Q8	TRUE	TRUE	—	FALSE	—
Q9	FALSE	—	FALSE	—	—
Q10	TRUE	—	—	—	TRUE
Q11	FALSE	—	—	—	FALSE
Q12	TRUE	—	—	—	TRUE
Q13	FALSE	—	FALSE	—	—
Q14	TRUE	TRUE	—	—	—
Q15	FALSE	FALSE	—	—	—
Q16	FALSE	—	—	FALSE	—
Q17	FALSE	—	FALSE	—	—
Q18	TRUE	—	—	—	TRUE
Q19	FALSE	—	FALSE	—	—
Q20	TRUE	TRUE	—	—	—

Question	Total obsessional score	Checking	Washing	Slowness-repetition	Doubting-conscientiousness
Q21	FALSE	—	FALSE	—	—
Q22	FALSE	FALSE	—	—	—
Q23	FALSE	—	—	FALSE	—
Q24	FALSE	—	FALSE	—	—
Q25	FALSE	—	—	FALSE	—
Q26	TRUE	TRUE	TRUE	—	—
Q27	FALSE	—	FALSE	—	—
Q28	TRUE	TRUE	—	—	—
Q29	FALSE	—	—	FALSE	—
Q30	TRUE	—	—	—	TRUE

Appendix 5

ADDRESSES OF USEFUL ORGANIZATIONS

UK

British Association for Behavioural Psychotherapy
59 Revelstoke Road
Wimbledon Park
London SW18 5NJ

British Psychological Society
48 Princess Road East
Leicester LE1 7DR

Royal College of Psychiatrists
17 Belgrave Square
London SW1X 8PG

MIND, National Association for Mental Health
22 Harley Street
London W1N 2ED

Phobic Action
Claybury Grounds
Manor Road
Woodford Green
Essex 1G8 8PR

USA

The OCD Foundation, Inc.
PO Box 9573
New Haven
Connecticut 06535

The Anxiety Disorders Association of America
6000 Executive Boulevard
Suite 200
Rockville
Maryland 20852–3801

Appendix 6

SOME USEFUL READING

Technical

There are several technical books providing good accounts of obsessive-compulsive disorder. Here are a few:

Jenike, M.A., Baer, L., and Minichiello, W.E. (ed.) (1990). *Obsessive-compulsive disorders: theory and management*, 2nd edn. Year Book Medical Publishers, Chicago.
This edited volume gives useful up-to-date information on many aspects of the problems and discusses important theoretical issues.

Rachman, S.J. and Hodgson, R.J. (1980). *Obsessions and compulsions*. Prentice-Hall, Englewood Cliffs, NJ.
This book provides a description and discussion of the field of obsessive-compulsive disorder. It describes what is known about obsessions and compulsions, gives an account of the authors' research, and comments on theoretical issues.

Barlow, D.H. (1988). *Anxiety and its disorders*. Guilford Press, New York.
This is a comprehensive book on the whole range of anxiety disorders, and has a particularly useful chapter on obsessive-compulsive disorder.

For briefer accounts, see:

de Silva, P. (1987). Obsessions and compulsions: investigation and treatment. In *A handbook of clinical adult psychology* (ed. S.J.E. Lindsay and G.E. Powell), pp. 47-87. Gower, London.

Rachman, S.J. (1985). Obsessional-compulsive disorders. In *Psychological applications in psychiatry* (ed. B. Bradley and C. Thompson), pp. 7-39. Wiley, Chichester.

Steketee, G. and Foa, E.B. (1985). Obsessive–compulsive disorders. In *Clinical handbook of psychological disorders* (ed. D.H. Barlow), pp. 69–144. Guilford Press, New York.

An excellent account of behavioural treatment is found in:

Salkovskis, P. and Kirk, J. (1989). Obsessive–compulsive disorders. In *Cognitive behaviour therapy for psychiatric problems* (ed. K. Hawton, P. Salkovskis, J. Kirk, and D. Clark), pp. 129–68. Oxford University Press.

For a more detailed discussion of therapy, see:

Turner, S.M. and Beidel, D.C. (1988). *Treating obsessive–compulsive disorder*. Pergamon, New York.

For a discussion of theoretical approaches, see:

de Silva, P. (1988). Obsessive–compulsive disorder. In *Adult abnormal psychology* (ed. E. Miller and P.J. Cooper), pp. 194–217. Churchill Livingstone, Edinburgh.

Non-technical

Useful and readable accounts, including self-help advice, are found in the following books:

Greist, J.H. (1989). *Obsessive–compulsive disorder: a guide*. University of Wisconsin Press. Available from: Anxiety-Disorders Clinic, Department of Psychiatry, University of Wisconsin, 600 Highland Avenue, Madison, Wisconsin 53792.

Greist, J.H., Jefferson, J.W., and Marks, I.M. (1986). *Anxiety and its treatment*. American Psychiatric Press, Inc., Washington, DC.

For an excellent personal account of obsessive–compulsive phenomena, especially obsessional thoughts, see:

Toates, F. (1990). *Obsessional thoughts and behaviour*. Thornsons, Wellingborough.

Index